THE LIFE AND WORDS OF
St. Francis of Assisi

P9-DDJ-005

Other books by the author available from
Scholastic Book Services

THE BATTLE OF BRITAIN

THE LIFE AND WORDS OF MARTIN LUTHER KING, JR.

THE NEW SOUND/YES (editor)

PATTON

THE LAST CZAR

THE LIFE AND WORDS OF JESUS CHRIST (in preparation)

*A NATION CONCEIVED AND DEDICATED (coauthor)

*OLD HATE—NEW HOPE (coauthor)

*BETWEEN TWO WARS (coauthor)

*YESTERDAY, TODAY, TOMORROW (coauthor)

*from *American Adventures*—U.S. history from Colonial times to the present.

THE LIFE AND WORDS OF
St. Francis of Assisi

by **IRA PECK**

Consultant: Rev. Fr. Marion A. Habig, O.F.M.

Illustrated by DOROTHY D'ANNA

SCHOLASTIC BOOK SERVICES
New York Toronto London Auckland Sydney Tokyo

This book is sold subject to the condition that it shall not be resold, lent, or otherwise circulated in any binding or cover other than that in which it is published—unless prior written permission has been obtained from the publisher—and without a similar condition, including this condition, being imposed on the subsequent purchaser.

Copyright © 1973 by Scholastic Magazines, Inc. All rights reserved. Published by Scholastic Book Services, a division of Scholastic Magazines, Inc.

1st printing .... September 1973
Printed in the U.S.A.

CONTENTS

To my wife, Virginia,
for her patience and wise counsel

Preface–
A Very Human Saint

ow do you picture St. Francis of Assisi in your mind's eye? Do you see him, perhaps, the way so many artists have portrayed him, as a soulful-looking man, his eyes lifted gently and piously toward heaven, his arms outstretched in solitary prayer? If this quite real image of St. Francis has nonetheless become almost a stereotype, one cannot fault the artists who helped create it. For they were trying to convey the deeply spiritual nature of the man, and this attitude of contemplation was for them the very essence of spirituality.

In a sense, however, they may have done Francis a disservice. For Francis had many very human as well as ethereal qualities, and in his own lifetime he reproved those who were already proclaiming him a saint. Though he was an ascetic, he was until the last years of his life a very cheerful man, and he regarded mirth and joy as a religious duty. He rebuked those friars who appeared gloomy or sombre, saying, "Let those who belong to the Devil hang their heads — we ought to be glad and rejoice in the Lord."

Though he often fasted himself, or spread ashes over his food to lessen his enjoyment of it, he chided those brothers who fasted *excessively* because, he said, "The Lord wants converts, not victims." He wrote joyous hymns that he and the brothers used to sing in towns, and he liked to call his Order "The *Jongleurs* [Minstrels] of God." He loved nature ardently and called all of God's creatures his brothers and sisters. His first biographer, Brother Thomas of Celano, tells us that Francis "forbade the brethren to cut down the whole tree when they needed wood, so that it might have hope of sprouting again. . . . He commanded that a little place be set aside in the garden for sweet-smelling and flowering plants. . . . He removed little worms from the road, lest they be crushed under foot. . . . He ordered that honey and warm wine be set out for the bees lest they perish from want in the cold of winter." Surely Francis must have been one of the very first ecologists.

For all his gentleness, he was a plucky little

man, and he was not easily rebuffed by anyone, including princes of the Church. Yet from Popes to peasants, sultans to outcasts, he loved and respected all men, reserving for the poor, in whom he saw the image of Christ, the greatest devotion. Born to wealth, he renounced all material possessions and chose himself to lead a life of poverty.

Apart from his love of nature, does the life of this very human saint have any meaning for us today? In many ways, Francis expressed in his own time, and in his own youth, the feelings of so many of today's young people. His message, which he preached everywhere in homely but touching words, was a call to peace, gentleness, simplicity, love of God and all His creatures, and a warning not to place one's trust in worldly riches.

Francis rejected materialism as a goal of life, and by his own example of poverty and holiness inspired a great many people of his time to live simpler and purer lives, giving their wealth and their energies to the care of the poor and the sick, and renouncing violence. It was an example not only for his generation, but for all generations. For today's youth especially, in its earnest striving for a more spiritual ideal, Francis' life will touch a sympathetic chord.

The Master of Revels

The town of Assisi, where Francis lived more than 700 years ago, is not much different today than it was in his time. It lies on a hillside in a mountainous area of central Italy called Umbria. Like so many medieval hill towns, its streets are narrow, winding, and very steep. The centuries-old houses that line the streets are made of a rose-colored stone that gives a soft, warm cast to the entire town.

In one such house, in the year 1182, a son was born to Pietro (Peter) di Bernardone, a wealthy cloth merchant, and his wife, Pica. Pietro was on a business trip in France at the time his first son was born, and in his absence Pica had the boy baptized Giovanni (John). On his return, however, Pietro chose to call the boy Francesco (Francis) — literally "Frenchman" — probably because of his admiration for the country he had just visited. At this time, Francis was quite an unusual name. It is possible, though not certain, that Pica herself was French, and that Pietro had met and courted her on an earlier business trip. In any event, Francis was taught to speak French, and in time he developed a great fondness for the poetry and songs of France as well as its language. Later they would inspire him with dreams of chivalry and knighthood that he tried in vain to fulfill.

Francis' formal education, like that of most boys of his time, was limited. He went to school at the Church of San Giorgio where the priests taught him reading, writing, and some Latin. He never really became very proficient in writing, and in later years he preferred to dictate his letters. At an early age, Francis was already assisting his father in his shop.

There was little in Francis' youth to indicate that he was destined for the religious life. On the contrary, according to Thomas of Celano, his behavior was quite scandalous. Brother Thomas called him "the master of revels" in Assisi, which is a 13th-century way of saying that he was the town's leading playboy. He spent money extravagantly, dressed like a dandy, engaged in all kinds of pranks, and attracted a group of worthless followers, mainly young members of the nobility who "sponged" off him. With these friends, Francis drank and went to parties almost nightly. Thomas of Celano tells us that until Francis was almost twenty-five, "he wasted his time miserably. Indeed, he outdid all others in vanities, in jokes, in strange doings, in idle and useless talk, in songs, in soft and flowing garments, for he was very rich and not a hoarder of money but a squanderer of his possessions."

His father was quite a frugal man, and sometimes he would admonish Francis, saying, "Anyone would think you were a nobleman's son, and not the son of a simple merchant." Yet Pietro made no effort to curb Francis' spending, and it is quite possible that inwardly he took some pride in the fact that his son, a member of the merchant middle class, counted as his friends the sons of the nobility. Pica, who was a gentle woman, no doubt was upset over her son's escapades, but she too was inclined to indulge him. When neighbors called attention to his carousing at night, she would only reply, "I am sure that some day he will become a good Christian."

How can one account for Francis' frivolous behavior as a youth? Most likely it was influenced by the French troubadours of his time. These poets and musicians traveled all over France and Italy with their guitars, singing of the romantic and heroic exploits of noble knights. It was the beginning of the Age of Chivalry, when knighthood was being idealized in songs, poems, and legends. Francis developed a passion for chivalry early in his life, and probably he threw himself into dissipation in the belief that this was the way that gallant young noblemen were supposed to act. Yet his passion for chivalry had some redeeming features. Courtesy and good manners were an essential part of chivalry, and Francis was unfailingly courteous to all. It was one of the traits that distinguished him throughout his life. Generosity was also an essential part of chivalry, and if Francis spent a great deal of money on worthless friends, he was also very open-handed with the poor.

One day, however, Francis did something that was quite uncharacteristic of him. While he was serving some customers in his father's shop, a beggar came in and asked for alms " for the love of God." Because he was busy, Francis became impatient with the beggar and sent him away rudely. A moment later he was conscience-stricken. "If this man had asked for money for one of your noble friends," he said to himself, "you would have been proud to give it to him. Yet when he asked for money in the name of God, you sent him away!" Leaving his customers, Francis ran out into the street and pressed some money into the beggar's hand.

When Francis was only 20 years old, he got his first chance to indulge his dreams of chivalry. In 1202, a war broke out between Assisi and its much larger neighbor, Perugia. (In the Middle Ages, independent Italian city-states fought against each other constantly.) All male Assisians from 18 to 60 were required to serve in the army. Because of his wealth, Francis was able to outfit himself with a horse and armor and serve in the cavalry, a privilege that was formerly reserved only for members of the nobility.

The war between the two cities, a series of sporadic but fierce skirmishes that endured until 1210, tells us a great deal about Francis' times. In the 12th and 13th centuries, northern Italian cities and towns were struggling to free themselves of foreign rule. The foreign power that dominated them was the Holy Roman Empire, which consisted mainly of present-day Germany, Austria, Bohemia, and Switzerland. In Rome, the Popes were engaged in a struggle of their own with the Holy Roman (German) Emperors, for the political domination of all Europe. As a consequence, the Papacy and the towns of northern Italy were often allied against the German emperors.

During Francis' youth, Assisi too was caught up in these struggles. Assisi was then ruled by a German overlord, Conrad of Swabia, Duke of Spoleto, whose fortress-castle dominated the entire town from atop its hill. The Assisians had no love for this petty German tyrant — they nicknamed him "Old Nit-Wit." Then, in 1198, a new Pope endowed with strong leadership qualities, Innocent III, was enthroned in Rome, and Duke Conrad's days were numbered. Innocent ordered Conrad to turn over Assisi to his authority. He was required to go to Narni and there pay homage to the Pope's representatives. No sooner was Conrad on the road to Narni than the Assisians besieged his castle, overcame its German defenders, and then proceeded to dismantle it stone by stone. Now, to protect their newly won independence against both the Emperor and Pope (or anyone else), the Assisians swiftly built a defensive wall around the town, using the stones torn from Conrad's castle. Francis was 17 at this time, and it is very likely that he took part in the building of the wall, parts of which are still standing today.

The citizens of the free commune of Assisi were beginning to feel their oats. Having overthrown the foreign tyrant, Conrad, they now began to tilt with the local tyrants, the members of the feudal nobility whose castles generally were situated outside the town's walls. These counts and barons were particularly irksome to the citizens of Assisi, placing heavy road tolls on their trade and demanding the fulfillment of ancient services that the townspeople found odious. Now the free citizens' militia began tearing down the castles of the local nobility too. The nobles appealed to Assisi's old enemy, Perugia, for help. Perugia, looking for an opportunity to impose its rule on Assisi, answered the call. It declared war on Assisi in 1202. The citizen army of Assisi, together with those members of the nobility who had remained loyal to the town, met the troops of Perugia on the plain between the two cities. The Assisians were routed, many of them slain (along with their horses), and many more were taken prisoner. Among the prisoners taken was Francis. Because of his noble appearance, the young cloth merchant's son was not held captive with the common citizens, but was confined instead with the noble prisoners.

At best, it was a dreary, miserable confinement, yet Francis astonished his fellow prisoners by remaining relentlessly cheerful throughout it. Instead of cursing his luck or groaning like the others, he sang or joked, and some of the prisoners undoubtedly thought he was mad. When anyone asked him what he was so cheerful about, he would reply, "How can I be sad when I think of the great future that awaits me, and how I shall be the idol of the whole world?"

Francis' reply was not in any sense a prophecy of the religious vocation that one day would bring him both fame and adoration. At this time, he was still dreaming of glorious military adventures that would lead eventually to his being dubbed a knight, which to him was the greatest honor imaginable.

A year later, a temporary peace was concluded between Assisi and Perugia. Francis, now 21, was free to go home.

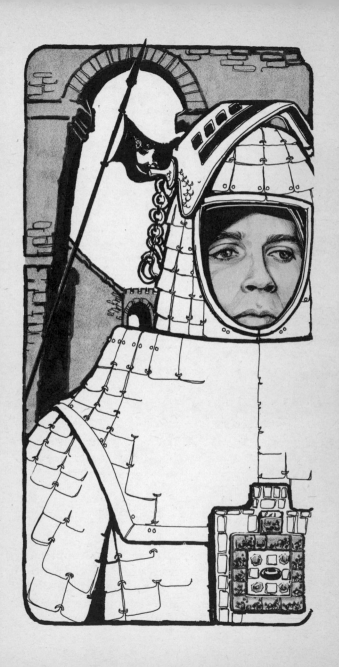

The Search
for a Higher Truth

rancis quickly resumed his role as "master of revels" in Assisi, plunging into a feverish whirl of pleasure-seeking. Perhaps he overdid it, or perhaps his health had been weakened by imprisonment. In any event, soon afterward he became gravely ill, and for weeks he hovered near death. Gradually, however, he began to recover, yet it was apparent that the long physical crisis had produced a profound change in him emotionally. One day, when he felt well enough to go outdoors, he took a walk toward one of the city's gates. From this gate there is a magnificent view of the plain below Assisi with its beautiful vineyards and olive groves and, in the distance, the snow-capped peaks of the Apennine mountains. Francis hoped that this view would help restore his spirits, filling him with the same delight it always had before his illness. Instead, he felt only a sense of depression as he reflected on the emptiness and uselessness of his former life.

Francis had begun to change, yet it was difficult for him to forego his old habits. At this time, he really didn't know any other way of life. As his strength returned, he once again took up the pursuit of pleasure, although he now found less and less enjoyment in it. Then, one day, an opportunity for military adventure and glory was again presented to Francis. Pope Innocent III was waging war against the forces of the Holy Roman Emperor in the south of Italy. His armies were led by an illustrious soldier, Duke Walter of Brienne. The Germans were thoroughly hated in Italy, and a wave of patriotic feeling swept over the Italian peninsula. In Assisi, a nobleman had decided to raise a troop of men to join Duke Walter's forces. For Francis, it was the answer to his dreams of knighthood and chivalry. He was sure that this time he would cover himself with glory in the fighting, and that Walter of Brienne would personally bestow knighthood on him. Francis threw himself into a frenzy of preparations, and his father spared no expense to outfit him with the most luxurious armor and equipment available. Francis' equipment, in fact, far outshone that of the nobleman who was to lead the expedition, and everyone spoke of it. Francis' joy was unbounded in those days, and he would exclaim to everyone he talked with, "I know that I am going to become a great prince!"

Yet before he left, Francis did something that may seem extraordinary, but really was quite in keeping with his generous, open nature. One of the noblemen who was to go on the expedition was quite poor — it may have been the leader but we do not know for sure — and his equipment was thoroughly forlorn. Out of simple kindness, Francis gave the nobleman his own costly armor and took the other's in exchange. Yet Francis' anticipation of glory was in no ways diminished. In a dream that night, he saw his father's shop filled not with bolts of cloth but with dazzling suits of armor, shields, weapons, and saddles, as though it were a knight's castle. He took it as a good omen.

At last the day of departure arrived and Francis rode off on horseback with the little troop of men that was to join Walter of Brienne in the south. Arriving in Spoleto on the road to Rome, however, Francis again fell ill. Racked with fever, he took to bed and spent a restless night. In this state, according to Thomas of Celano, he had another dream in which a voice admonished him to leave the expedition and serve the Lord, rather than a mere earthly vassal. The meaning of the dream, and what he was to do, he was told, would be made clearer to him when he returned home.

The next morning Francis saddled his horse and rode back to Assisi alone. It is not known what the reaction of his parents or the townspeople was on his return, but more than likely there was both keen disappointment and not a little laughter over his sudden about-face. It doesn't seem to have mattered. Before long, Francis' friends had again drawn him back into the old life, though he appears by now to have been quite fed up with it. More and more, he began to be withdrawn and to seek seclusion. Sometimes alone, or with one good friend in whom he confided, he would walk to a nearby mountain cave. Then he would enter it by himself and pray fervently for guidance. The meaningless rounds of festivities, the dreams of glory had palled on him. Clearly he was seeking to dedicate his life to a higher truth.

Though Francis still consorted occasionally with his pleasure-bent friends, and continued to spend money on them freely, they could not help notice the change that was coming over him. On one occasion in 1205, Francis invited them all to a very lavish banquet. There was a lot of good food and wine, and, as usual, his friends proclaimed him King of the Revels and otherwise flattered him. The banquet lasted far into the night, and when it was over, the revelers poured into the streets, singing and shouting. After awhile, however, they noticed that Francis was not among them. Some of them went back to look for him and found him standing alone in a street, lost in thought. One of them asked,

"What are you dreaming about, Francis? Are you thinking of taking a wife?"

Francis smiled and said, "Yes, I am thinking of taking a wife, but one more beautiful and more pure than any you could ever imagine."

Was Francis already thinking of leading a holy life in which he would take Lady Poverty for his bride? We cannot know for sure, but certainly that night proved to be an important turning point in Francis' life. From then on, he rejected his old friends and his old way of life completely. More and more he devoted himself to solitude, to prayer, and to helping the poor, with whom he now began to feel very close. He spent many of his days wandering alone in the fields, often deep in reverie. At home, or in town, he might drop whatever he was doing to enter a church and pray. If he passed a beggar in the street, he would give him all his money or, if he had no money, he would give him some of his clothes, including even his shirt. He thought too about poor priests and poor churches, and often sent them sacred objects anonymously.

Francis was of very little use to his father at this time, and Pietro was becoming increasingly annoyed and angry with his son. He could tolerate Francis spending his money on the sons of noblemen, but he found it intolerable that Francis was giving all his money to the poor. Yet the poor had become uppermost in Francis' mind. They had taken the place of his former friends, and now he felt something like kinship to them. "The truth was," Brother Thomas wrote, "that he had become one of them, thinking only of sharing their life of privations."

Perhaps it was this desire to experience poverty himself that led Francis to make a pilgrimage to Rome at this time. He had always given generously to beggars, but what, he asked himself, was it like to be a beggar oneself? Could he endure poverty? He wanted to know how it felt to have nothing, and to depend for his bread on the charity or whim of others. In Rome, where no one knew him, he might have the opportunity to find out.

Francis first visited St. Peter's Church, where it was the custom for pilgrims to throw coins through the grated window of the Apostle's tomb. He was both surprised and pained by the paltry offerings of the pilgrims that day. In keeping with his chivalrous nature, he emptied his purse of all its coins, gold and otherwise, and tossed them through the grating, a gesture that astonished the others.

Outside the church was the usual crowd of beggars asking for alms. This was the opportunity that Francis had been looking for. He approached one of the beggars and offered to exchange clothes with him. The offer was readily accepted, and a short time later Francis was standing on the steps of the church dressed in rags, begging for alms with all the others. He did this all day, and apparently experienced great joy from it. One biographer tells us that Francis begged in French, the language he always used when he was very happy.

Francis had passed what he felt was a great test. He had worn rags and eaten a beggar's meal and found that poverty had brought him contentment. When he returned home, he prayed more and more for guidance and light. Soon after, the light came to him in an experience he had with lepers. It was the final step in his conversion to a holy life.

As a youth, Francis had always had a terrible aversion to victims of leprosy, who were then fairly numerous in Europe. He was not unique in his aversion. The putrefying flesh, open sores, and dreadful odor produced by this disease made its victims terribly repulsive. They were shunned by all but a handful of pious souls, the Knights of Lazarus, who cared for them in hospitals.

One day Francis was out riding when he saw a leper walking in the road a short distance away. In the past, Francis would have spun his horse around and galloped away as fast as possible. He was tempted to gallop away this time too, but he managed to control himself. Then, dismounting from his horse, he approached the leper, embraced him, and pressed some coins into his hand. Francis was so elated by this victory over himself that the next day he visited a nearby lepers' hospital. From all the cells the sick came out to meet this curiosity. They gathered around the former dandy, and he saw their half-destroyed faces, their swollen, decaying limbs, and their sometimes fingerless hands. For a few moments, Francis thought he would be overcome by nausea. But again he was able to control himself, and he proceeded to hand out money to the lepers and to kiss each one on the hand. The gratitude felt by these patients toward their visitor was no greater than the happiness that Francis felt within himself. Francis described this experience in his Last Will and Testament:

"During my life of sin," he wrote, "nothing disgusted me like seeing victims of leprosy. It was the Lord Himself who urged me to go to them. I did so, and ever since everything was so changed for me that what had seemed at first painful and impossible to overcome became easy and pleasant. Shortly after, I definitely forsook the world [to take up the religious life]."

Francis Breaks
with His Father

The bitterness that Pietro di Bernardone felt toward his son, Francis, was becoming deeper with each passing day. At best, he saw Francis as disobedient; at worst, he suspected him of being a lunatic. Even Pica could not calm him when he began to upbraid his son. As for Francis, he now had only one wish — to flee this house where, instead of love, he found only reproaches and anguish. A break between the father and son was becoming inevitable. It took place finally in 1207, a short time after Francis' visit to the leper hospital.

Dotting the countryside around Assisi were numerous small churches, or chapels, that Francis liked to visit in his wanderings. One of these rustic chapels, San Damiano, was at this time virtually a ruin. It was tended only by one poor priest who subsisted on whatever alms occasionally came his way. The inside of the chapel contained only an altar of stones above which hung a large Byzantine cross with the figure of Christ painted on it. Unlike most renditions of the crucifixion that stress Christ's suffering, His expression in this painting is one of great calm and gentleness. One early spring day, Francis entered this chapel and prayed, as he so often did at this time, for guidance.

"Grant me, O Lord, to know thee so well," Francis asked, "that in all things I may act by thy light and in accordance with thy holy will."

From the crucifix there came a voice, one that Francis heard within his heart, which said to him, "Francis, go repair My house, which is falling in ruins."

The effect that these words had on Francis was impossible for him to describe. One can only imagine the elation he felt that God had at last spoken to him and answered his prayers. Yet what did the message really mean? Was it an exhortation to rescue the Church, which was then being assailed on all sides by heretics and self-appointed reformers? Francis was essentially a very simple, unlettered youth. Looking about him, he saw the crumbling condition of the chapel and interpreted the words he had heard quite literally — the job that God had given him was to rebuild the chapel.

With all his devotion and enthusiasm, Francis began at once to comply with the Lord's directions. The first thing he did was to give the priest who tended the chapel some money for a lamp and oil to burn before the crucifix. The job of repairing the chapel would, of course, require a great deal more money. Where was Francis to get it? He had no trouble finding the answer. He hurried home, picked out some of his father's most expensive bolts of cloth, and loaded them on a horse. Then he rode off to a neighboring town where he proceeded to sell both the cloth and his horse. Returning to the chapel of San Damiano on foot, Francis handed the priest the money he had gotten and told him to use it to restore the little church. At this the priest balked. He knew Francis quite well — perhaps this was just another one of his pranks. He also knew Francis' father. Pietro di Bernardone was an important man in Assisi, and he had no wish to offend him by accepting such a large sum of money from Francis. Quite probably he also had his suspicions about how Francis had obtained the money. In the end, despite Francis' pleading, the priest refused the offering. Francis did persuade him, however, to let him live for a while at San Damiano to devote himself to prayer.

Pietro was away on business while these events were taking place. When he returned and found his son gone and bolts of cloth as well as a horse missing, he flew into a rage. He soon found out where Francis was, and with a group of friends and neighbors, rushed to San Damiano to bring Francis home by force, if necessary. As soon as Francis heard them coming, he hid himself in a nearby cave and Pietro was unable to find him. He remained hidden in the cave for a month until at last he resolved to face his father and headed back to town.

One can imagine his appearance as he walked through the streets of Assisi that day. After a month in a cave, with very little food, he was pale and emaciated, his face unshaven, his hair long and dishevelled, and his clothes in tatters. On seeing this ragged figure who was once so elegant, a crowd of Assisians began to follow him through the streets shouting taunts and insults. Children threw stones and mud at him and screamed, "A madman! A madman!" As the crowd drew nearer his house, Pietro di Bernardone went out into the street to see what all the shouting was about. Then he saw his son, his first-born, for whom he had dreamed such great things, in this utterly wretched condition. Overcome simultaneously with sorrow, shame, and anger, Pietro seized his son and dragged him violently into the cellar of his house. There he locked Francis up in the darkness, but not before beating him and threatening to put him on a diet of bread and water. He was determined to break Francis to his will.

It is doubtful whether Francis would have broken under these conditions. He was no longer the spoiled dandy of former days, but a young man now of inflexible purpose. Fortunately, however, Francis' imprisonment did not last long. Pietro again left town on a business trip, and Pica attempted in his absence to sway her son by more gentle means than Pietro had used. Seeing that her pleading was quite useless, and unable to see her son suffer any further, she set him free. It was a courageous act, for she well knew Pietro's temper. Francis immediately went back to his refuge at San Damiano.

On his return to Assisi, Pietro must have realized the futility of trying to browbeat Francis into submission. Now he resolved on a new strategy. He would take his son to court, charging him with the theft of his goods. His object probably was to have the court banish Francis from Assisi so that Pietro, a respectable citizen, would be spared any further embarrassment from his son. He may also have sought to disinherit him. At the very least, he hoped to get back the money that Francis had obtained from the sale of his goods. Pietro di Bernardone carried a lot of weight in Assisi — officially he was "a benefactor and guardian of the republic" — and he was confident the magistrates would act in his favor.

Summoned before the city magistrates, Francis boldly proclaimed that the court had no jurisdiction over him. It was, he said, a civil court and he, as a servant of God, could only be tried by a Church tribunal. It is doubtful whether Francis had any official status as a clergyman at this time, as some biographers have theorized. Most likely he was still a layman, though he felt a strong religious calling. The case, however, was a kind of hot potato for the magistrates. Pietro was a wealthy and influential man, but Francis may have had some support from the Bishop of Assisi. The magistrates therefore seemed only too willing to accept Francis' argument, and advised Pietro that he would have to take his case to the bishop's court.

On the appointed day, both Francis and his father appeared before Bishop Guido of Assisi for the hearing. The proceedings took place in the piazza before the bishop's palace, and a large crowd turned out to witness the case of the wealthy cloth merchant against his "crazy" son. Bishop Guido appears to have been quite sympathetic to Francis, but he could not, of course, condone the theft of Pietro's goods. Though Francis claimed that the money he had gotten for the cloth was now Church property, the bishop ordered him to return it to his father, saying, "If you would serve the Church, you have no right, under color of good works, to keep money obtained in this way. So give back such wrongly acquired goods to your father, to appease him."

"My Lord," Francis replied to the bishop, "I will not only give him the money cheerfully, but I will do more."

Then Francis made an extraordinary gesture, one that has inspired poets and painters for centuries. He went inside the bishop's palace, and when he reappeared in the square a few moments later, he was stark naked, holding all his clothes in his hands. Turning to the crowd he shouted, "Listen, all of you, to what I have to say! Up to now, I have called Pietro di Bernardone my father. But now I propose to serve God. Therefore I return to Pietro his money and all the clothes I got from him so that hereafter I shall not say, 'My father, Pietro di Bernardone,' but 'Our Father who art in heaven!' "

With this, Francis threw his clothes and his purse on the ground before his father. As Pietro picked them up and stalked off angrily, the crowd began to murmur in astonishment, and many openly wept in sympathy for Francis. Bishop Guido then drew Francis within his arms and covered the shivering young man with his cape.

With one symbolic gesture, Francis had renounced his father, his home, and all his rights as son and heir. It was the most decisive act of his life, committing him irrevocably to the service of God.

Singing for Stones,
Begging for Bread

Covered only with an old gardener's cloak that the bishop had given him, Francis left Assisi to find solitude in the nearby mountains, taking the road that leads up Mount Subasio. It was April 1207, and although there was still some snow clinging to the mountainside, the sun was warm and Francis felt exhilarated by the beauty of the day. As was his habit when he was especially happy, he sang hymns of praise (in French) to God, sometimes employing melodies derived from the troubadours. As night began to fall, his singing attracted the attention of a band of robbers hiding out on the wooded mountain. The robbers rushed him, but were disappointed with their penniless victim wearing such a shabby cloak.

"Who are you?" they asked. "I am the herald of the great King," Francis replied quite matter-of-factly. The robbers promptly grabbed him by the arms and legs and threw him into a ditch filled with snow. "Lie there, you peasant who wants to play at being God's herald!" they shouted to him, and then departed.

With some difficulty, Francis raised himself out of the ditch and then continued wandering over the mountain, singing as before. After awhile Francis came to a small Benedictine monastery where he offered to work in the kitchen. Francis hoped that in exchange for his labor the monks would give him some clothes. They not only gave him no clothes, but they gave him so little food that after a few days he had to leave. In later years, the prior of the monastery begged Francis' forgiveness for this shabby treatment, and it was readily given.

Francis now proceeded to the town of Gubbio where an old friend provided him with some clothes. The outfit that Francis assumed was the typical hermit's garb of the time — a tunic with a belt around the waist, sandals, and a walking stick. Then he went to live for a while at a lepers' hospital where he cared for the patients, washing and dressing their sores, and cheering them with his presence.

Buoyed by his experience at the hospital, Francis now returned to San Damiano to begin the work of rebuilding. Where was he to get the means to accomplish it? Francis found the answer in singing and begging. He began to appear in the squares and marketplaces of Assisi, singing his hymns based on the latest troubadour melodies. He became, in effect, a kind of minstrel himself. After each song he would beg his listeners for stones, saying with a smile, "He who gives me a stone will have his reward in heaven." Some people laughed at him and were convinced that he was mad. Others, however, moved by the sight of this once wealthy playboy who had turned beggar, helped him. Though Francis was rather short and slightly built, he carried away the stones himself and joyfully began restoring San Damiano.

To express his gratitude to Francis, the priest there began waiting on him, preparing for him the best meals he could. After awhile this began to embarrass Francis. He was not only imposing on the priest an expense he could ill afford, but he felt he was not truly living as a pauper. He resolved, therefore, to beg for his meals too. The next day at noon, while the people of Assisi were sitting down to lunch Francis went from door to door with a bowl in his hand, asking for food. What he received was hardly very appetizing — mostly stale bread and leftover scraps that probably would have been tossed into the garbage pail. The sight of this pathetic mixture in his bowl almost turned Francis' stomach, but he forced himself to eat it. Afterwards, however, he felt much the same sense of gratification as when he had first embraced a leper.

It was by no means easy for Francis to beg at first. Occasionally he would meet his father, who would shower him with curses. Many others taunted him, including his younger brother, Angelo. One wintry day the two brothers met in church. Seeing Francis shivering as he knelt in prayer, Angelo said quite loudly to a friend, "Go and ask Francis if he will not sell you a penny's worth of sweat." Francis had a ready answer. "I prefer," he said, "to keep it for God, who will give me a much better price for it than you."

On another occasion, when Francis was begging for oil for the lamp at San Damiano, he came to a house where a party was going on. Francis looked inside and recognized many of his former friends. Ashamed to appear before them as a beggar, he started to leave, but then he despised himself even more for being a coward. Returning to the house, he entered it and pleaded earnestly for the needed oil, but not before confessing the weakness he had felt at first.

Francis restored San Damiano between 1207–1208 and soon was repairing other nearby churches that were in a state of decay. At the same time, he continued to care for lepers. He probably worked on the Church of St. Peter, which was then outside of Assisi's walls, and finally began restoring a little chapel that later was to become the cradle of the Franciscan movement. Located on the plain below Assisi, this chapel was very old, and was reputed to have been built by pilgrims on their return from the Holy Land in the year 352. Its name was St. Mary of the Angels, but it was better known as the *Portiuncula* — literally, the little portion of earth. In Francis' time, according to Thomas of Celano, it was "deserted and cared for by no one. When the holy man of God [Francis] saw how it was thus in ruins, he was moved to pity because he burned with devotion toward the mother [Mary] of all good; and he began to live there in great zeal."

Apparently Francis fell in love with this little chapel surrounded by woods. At that time, he saw his vocation simply as the restoration of old and dilapidated churches. Beyond that, he wished only a life of quiet meditation and solitude, taking care of the Portiuncula and on occasion inviting a priest there to say Mass. His life, however, would soon change quite dramatically. On February 24, 1208, he was listening to Mass at the restored Portiuncula. It was the festival day of St. Matthias, and the priest began to read from the Gospel the passage in which Jesus spoke to his apostles as follows:

"Go and preach the message, 'The Kingdom of Heaven is at hand.' Heal the sick, cleanse the lepers, cast out devils. Freely have you received, freely give. Do not possess gold nor silver, nor money in your purse, nor scrip for your journey, nor two coats, nor shoes, nor a staff, for the laborer deserves a living.

"And whatever city or town you enter, inquire who in it is worthy, and there abide until you leave. And when you go into the house, salute it, saying, 'Peace be to this house.' "

These words struck Francis as nothing less than a divine revelation. He believed that God

43

was telling him that he should live exactly as one of Christ's apostles according to the Gospel. This meant that he must go out into the world and preach in utter poverty, seeking converts for Christ.

Francis was overjoyed by this revelation and exclaimed to the priest who had read the passage, "This is what I long to do with all my soul! From this day on, I shall set myself to practice it with all my strength."

Almost immediately, as if to obey this new commandment, he threw away his outer coat, his belt, for which he substituted a piece of cord, his purse, his sandals, and his staff. He was ready to observe literally the words of the Bible. Francis the church restorer and hermit was to become Francis the evangelist.

Francis Wins
Some Converts

The next morning Francis went up to Assisi and began to preach in the streets. In his appearance, he was anything but imposing. He was small and quite plain-looking, dressed in a coarse gray tunic that resembled burlap, and barefoot. Neither was he an eloquent speechmaker — his words were quite simple and artless. Yet undoubtedly these were his greatest assets as a preacher. The sight of this young man who had chosen a life of poverty and ministering to lepers, combined with his unaffected words that seemed to come straight from the heart, touched his listeners deeply. This simplicity was something new to them. They had never before heard sermons preached in the streets. They were used to hearing them in the great churches, and usually in Latin which few of them could understand.

Francis' greeting to all was, "The Lord give you peace!" In his sermons, he spoke of peace as the greatest good for man — peace with God by keeping his commandments, peace with one's fellow men by upright conduct, and peace with oneself by having a good conscience. The people who only a year before had laughed at him now began to look upon him almost with reverence. Some were even boasting of this "holy man" in their midst. He would be affectionately dubbed by them *Il Poverello* — the Little Poor Man.

Before long Francis began to attract a small group of disciples. The first we know of were Bernard of Quintavalle and Peter of Catani. Both men were solid citizens, Bernard a well-to-do merchant, Peter a prominent lawyer. Bernard was impressed with Francis' example in renouncing his wealth, and felt a strong impulse to follow him in the religious life. According to legend, before Bernard would definitely commit himself, he wanted to test Francis' piety. Was Francis truly a man of prayer? Or was he a fraud? Bernard therefore invited Francis to sleep one night in his own room where a lamp usually burned all evening. If Francis really prayed, Bernard would be able to see him.

That night both men pretended to fall fast asleep. Hearing Bernard's feigned snoring and convinced that he was in a deep slumber, Francis got up and prayed ardently most of the night. Bernard needed no further convincing. In the morning he expressed the wish to join Francis in renouncing the world. The story has at least some basis in truth, for Brother Thomas of Celano tells us briefly that "Bernard saw Francis praying at night, sleeping little, praising God and His Mother, the Blessed Virgin."

Bernard expressed his wish to join Francis in the form of a question: "What would you say a man should do who wanted to get rid of his money?" Francis replied that the answer would have to be found by consulting the Gospels. The next morning, Francis, Bernard, and Peter entered the Church of St. Nicholas and prayed. Then Francis went up to the altar, opened the book of Gospels, and found the following words: "If you will be perfect, sell what you have and give to the poor." The second time he opened the book he found these words: "If any man wishes to come after Me, let him deny himself and take up his cross and follow Me." The third time, Francis found these words: "And He commanded them that they take nothing for their journey." These sentences seemed to Francis a confirmation of the revelation he had already received at the Portiuncula. He then told Bernard and Peter, "Brothers, this is the life and the Rule [charter] for us, and all who may want to join our company in the future. Go, therefore, and comply with what you have heard."

Both men immediately sold all their property and distributed the proceeds among the poor.

We do not know how Peter disposed of his wealth, but Bernard handed out his considerable fortune to the poor on the steps of the Church of San Giorgio. Francis stood beside him as he did so. Soon Francis was approached by a priest named Sylvester who had once sold him some stones at a modest price when he was working to restore churches. Seeing the large sums of money being given away by Bernard, Sylvester reproached Francis for having paid so little for his stones. Francis was angered by this display of greed. Taking a handful of coins from Bernard's pockets, he thrust them at Sylvester, saying, "Here, are you satisfied now?" One can imagine Sylvester's embarrassment as the crowd on the church steps murmured its disapproval. The incident must have affected Sylvester deeply, for some time later he too renounced his goods and became one of Francis' most devoted followers.

The news that two of its most prominent citizens, Bernard and Peter, had chosen to join Francis in a life of holy poverty traveled fast around Assisi and the neighboring countryside. Only about a week later, a simple, unlettered farmer's son named Giles who, according to legend was "troubled about his salvation," sought out Francis near the Portiuncula. Seeing Francis emerge from the woods, Giles threw himself at his feet and begged to be received into his small company.

"Dear Brother," said Francis, "God has shown you a wonderful favor. Had the Emperor come to Assisi and chosen you as a knight, you would feel proud indeed. How much more should you rejoice that God has chosen you to serve him as a true knight in our little band?"

Taking Giles by the hand, he led him to the little hut that he, Bernard, and Peter had built near the Portiuncula and presented him to the others. "Here," he said, "is a good brother whom God has sent us. Let us sit down and eat to celebrate his coming." Giles' gentle nature endeared him to Francis. It wasn't long before Francis, who was thoroughly familiar with the legend of King Arthur and his court, began to call Giles his "Knight of the Round Table."

In theory, the little hut near the Portiuncula was the home of Francis and his three brothers. In reality, however, it was little more than an occasional meeting place. At this time, they traveled around the countryside in pairs, singing and preaching in the town squares, and earning their bread by helping the peasants in the fields. They went wherever their fancy took them, sleeping in haylofts, in leper hospitals, or even under the porches of churches. Francis was not yet celebrated as a preacher, and he limited himself at this time to singing a few songs in the public squares, after which he would urge his few listeners to love God above all else and to repent of their sins. When Francis would finish, Giles, who was not much of a speaker himself, would simply add, "Whatever he says is true! Do everything he tells you!"

Francis and the brothers were not very successful with their preaching outside of Assisi during these early days. Most people distrusted them. Who were these odd-looking men dressed in rags who came to them with their songs and sermons? When the brothers replied that they belonged to no particular monastic order but were simply "penitents from the city of Assisi," it was not very reassuring. Young women, frightened by their appearance, often ran away when they saw them coming. Perhaps a few people saw them as holy men, but the great majority considered them fanatics, fools, or even lunatics.

Francis remained optimistic, and later confided to his disciples a vision in which he saw "a multitude of men coming toward us, asking that they might receive the habit of our holy religion. The sound of their footsteps coming from every country still echoes in my ears."

When Francis and his brothers returned to the Portiuncula, they were soon joined by four others, all of them from Assisi. This new development did not please the people of Assisi. It was one thing to give alms to Francis when *he* first began to beg. But now that he was gathering recruits, where would it end? How many of these healthy young men would they have to feed?

When the brothers went up to Assisi to beg from door to door, they were often turned away and insulted. "You have given away your own goods," the townspeople would tell them. "Now you want to live off others!"

Even Bishop Guido became alarmed at the increase in begging and felt compelled to talk to Francis about it.

"Your way of living," he told Francis, "without

owning anything, seems to me very hard and impractical."

Bishop Guido, in effect, was urging Francis to soften the rule which required all those who would join his company to live in absolute poverty. For Francis, however, this rule was the cornerstone of his movement. Both the letter and the spirit of the Scriptures proclaimed to him the holiness of poverty. Hadn't Jesus himself been poor and accepted charity? Hadn't Jesus said, "What shall it profit a man if he gains the world and loses his soul?"

In Francis' time, there were already many who believed that the full enjoyment of life depended upon having many possessions. Francis, inspired by the example of Jesus and the Apostles, believed the contrary to be true. He believed that the fewer possessions one had, the freer one was to serve God and to enjoy the treasures of nature, in which he saw God's creation. Possessions were entrapments, and the greatest obstacles to love and peace. According to Thomas of Celano, "There was no one so desirous of gold as Francis was desirous of poverty, and no one so solicitous in guarding his treasure as he was solicitous in guarding this pearl of the Gospel."

Francis' reply to Bishop Guido, therefore, was polite but uncompromising. "My Lord," he said, "if we possessed property, we should need arms to defend it. Property is the source of quarrels and lawsuits, and is an obstacle to the love of God and one's neighbor. This is why we do not desire any earthly goods."

Bishop Guido was not about to say that the Gospel was wrong, and declared himself convinced. Yet Francis himself knew that idleness and living solely on alms were dangerous too. Soon after, the brothers began hiring themselves out as manual laborers to earn their bread, and resorted to begging only when necessary.

Francis stated his philosophy regarding the importance of work in his Last Will and Testament. "I worked with my hands," he wrote, "and I firmly desire that all the other brothers work in some honest employment. Those who do not know a trade must learn one, not through desire to receive the price of their labor, but for example's sake and to repel idleness. And when the price of our labor is not given us, let us have recourse to the table of the Lord, begging alms from door to door." Francis had no shame at all about "eating at the table of the Lord." It was in keeping, he felt, with Christ's instructions to his Apostles, and an exercise in humility. He frequently called food obtained by begging "angel's bread."

Before long, Francis decided to undertake another preaching mission with his brothers. Francis told them that they were to preach peace and repentance "more by our example than by our words," and then warned them of the difficulties that lay ahead:

"You will find some men full of faith, gentleness, and goodness who will receive you and your words with joy. But you will find others, in greater numbers, faithless and proud, who will speak evil of you. Be resolute then to endure everything with patience and humility."

Francis' warning proved to be prophetic. Traveling in pairs again, the brothers were roughly treated by the townspeople whom they hoped to bring the message of peace and goodness. They were usually taken for thieves, madmen, or dangerous heretics, and driven away. Some people grabbed them by their hoods and dragged them on their backs through the streets, and in some places they were stripped of their clothes. The brothers made no effort to defend themselves, obeying the Gospel commandment to "resist not evil." The missions were not total failures, however, and Francis even succeeded in winning a new recruit for his group, a knight named Angelo Tancredi who seemed to Francis to be the fulfillment of all his youthful ideals.

The brothers returned to the Portiuncula at about the same time and quickly forgot the torments they had endured in the joy of their reunion. They were soon joined by four new recruits, bringing the group's number to 12. It was now time, Francis thought, to go to Rome and ask Pope Innocent III, the greatest religious and temporal leader of his time, to give the group his recognition and approval as a religious Order.

Francis Sways a Pope

The Church of the 13th century is often described as "all-powerful," its religious dominion unchallenged in Christendom, its political dominion accepted, willingly or unwillingly, by most kings and emperors. Yet at the time that Francis and his followers set out to see the Pope, in the spring of 1209, the Church was actually anything but omnipotent. It was then tottering under the assault of numerous large heretic sects, many of which were motivated by ideas of reform and Gospel poverty. These sects had sprung up largely as a reaction against the impiety and moral laxity that were then quite commonplace among clergymen. Many priests and monks were making a mockery of their vows in the pursuit of material comforts and pleasures, and in the neglect of their religious duties. Some high-ranking clergymen were living in unheard-of luxury, which they supported by selling church offices, even at public auctions. The evil of corruption was so widespread that Pope Innocent III, who was himself a reformer, said it "would take fire and sword to cure it."

Unlike most of the reformers of his time who wished a return to the poverty of the primitive Church, Francis was never attracted by heresy, nor did he ever denounce clergymen. He believed in the basic doctrines of the Church, and while he was not unaware of the failings of some clergymen, he thought that the best way of achieving reform was for him and his brothers to set an example for *all* the people of his time to aspire to as an ideal.

To a considerable extent, he was successful. It was Francis and his brothers, more than all the Papal letters of excommunication, who were responsible for ridding Italy and much of Europe of heresy, and bringing about a measure of reform. More than any other single figure, it was Francis who restored the Church in his time, not as a mason, which he originally believed to be his vocation, but as a nonviolent crusader.

Yet when Francis and his little group of penitents arrived in Rome to seek an audience with the Pope, how was Innocent or the members of his court, the Curia, to know that they were not just another sect of heretic reformers? Is it any wonder that the brothers met with considerable suspicion and doubt at first? Fortunately, Bishop Guido happened to be in Rome at this time, and he introduced them to a good friend of his in the Curia, Cardinal John of St. Paul, a man who enjoyed a reputation for outstanding piety. The Bishop assured Cardinal John that the brothers were not heretics, and had only the greatest reverence for the clergy.

Cardinal John was hospitable, but nevertheless he questioned Francis and his group cautiously for several days. His advice to them was not to attempt to found a new Order, but to join one of the older, established Orders. This Francis was unwilling to do, for many of these Orders owned considerable property and their monastics could live quite comfortably, even though as individuals they might personally own very little. Furthermore, these Orders fostered a cloistered life, and Francis wished above all to go out among the people to preach the message of the Gospel.

Francis was so persistent in defending his idea, and the loyalty of the brothers to the Church was so apparent, that Cardinal John was finally convinced. He agreed to speak to Pope Innocent and urge him to grant Francis and the brothers an audience. According to one account, Cardinal John told Innocent, "I have found a man of the highest perfection who wishes to live in conformity with the Holy Gospel. And I believe the Lord intends by him to renew the faith of the Church all over the world."

The next day the "Penitents from Assisi" were received by Innocent III and the Curia. Francis described his plans for an Order whose members would live and preach like the Apostles of old, in absolute poverty, and pleaded for the Pope's acceptance. Afterwards, some members of the Curia protested strenuously. To them, Francis and the brothers sounded all too much like one group of heretics who, before they were banned by the Church, had obtained permission to preach and had then stirred up the people against the clergy. Many members of the Curia also wondered how a religious Order could subsist without owning property or having a regular income. Apparently Pope Innocent had some doubts himself on this score, for he told the brothers, "My dear children, your life appears to me too severe. I do not doubt that all of you, borne up by your enthusiasm, are able to endure it. But we must think also of those who come after you, who may find your mode of life beyond their strength."

Cardinal John then took up the brothers' cause. "These men," he said, "only want us to allow them to live after the Gospel. If we reject this as impossible, then we are saying in effect that the Gospel cannot be practiced, and we insult Christ, who is the Author of the Gospel."

This argument made a strong impression on Pope Innocent. He called for another meeting with the brothers in a few days, when he would render his decision. Then he dismissed them, saying to Francis, "My son, pray God to manifest his will to us. When we know it, we shall be better prepared to give you an answer."

According to Thomas of Celano, Francis prayed during this interlude for help and received it in the form of a story related to him by Christ. When Francis next met with Innocent, he told the story to the Pope:

"Your Holiness," Francis said, "a poor but very beautiful woman once lived in the desert wilderness. A great king fell in love with her and married her in the hope she would bear him handsome sons. She did bear him many handsome sons, but they grew up penniless after the king returned to his court. When the sons were men, their mother said to the oldest ones, 'Do not be ashamed to be poor, for you are the king's sons. Go to his court, and he will give you all you need.'

"The king was struck by the handsome appearance of these young men and, seeing in them a resemblance to himself, asked them who their mother was. When they told him that she was a poor woman who lived in the desert, the king embraced them and said, 'Fear not, for you are my sons. And if I feed so many at my table, how much more should I feed you who are my lawful sons!' Then he sent word to their mother that she should send him all her sons that he might care for them too."

When Francis had finished the story, he explained its meaning to the Pope. "Your Holiness," he said, "the wilderness is the world, barren of virtue. This poor woman whom God made fruitful is me, to whom Christ has given sons who strive to reproduce the features of their father by imitating his poverty. Finally, the sons who sit at the table are my brothers, whom the Lord will never leave in need. For if he gives food to strangers, how much more will he give to his lawful children?"

This simple parable of poverty, told with so much earnestness by Francis, was intended to allay the Pope's fears about how the brothers would obtain their bread. At the same time, Francis was boldly asserting that he and his brothers were the *true* sons of Christ.

The story won Pope Innocent over. Francis was persistent, but obviously he was no heretic. He found inner joy in poverty, and wished only to share this joy with others. His zealousness for converts might possibly help the Church in its hour of peril. Brother Thomas tells us that shortly before this second meeting, Innocent had a dream in which he saw an ancient church leaning over, on the verge of collapsing in a heap of ruins. Suddenly a small, plain-looking man appeared and propped up the church with a push of his shoulders. Whether or not Pope Innocent actually had such a dream, it expresses symbolically what probably were his real feelings. The Church was tottering at the time. Innocent knew too that the pursuit of property by some members of the clergy was encouraging the heretic sects that beset the Church. Perhaps the Little Poor Man from Assisi was the agent of reform who would prevent it from toppling over.

Innocent decided to give Francis' Rule his approval, though it was both limited and tentative. The brothers were granted the right to preach repentance, that is to address simple moral sermons to the people, but this was not a general license to preach and expound doctrine. After the brothers swore to obey Francis, and Francis to obey the Pope, Innocent sent them off with these words:

"Go, brothers, and may God be with you. Preach penitence to everyone as the Lord reveals it to you! And if it pleases Him to increase your numbers, come back and tell me about it. Then I shall see about granting you more numerous favors and entrusting you with a more important mission."

This mission may have been to preach a crusade against either the Saracens or heretics. The favors probably meant the issuance of a Papal Bull (decree) that would officially recognize Francis' Rule, for so far Innocent had put nothing in writing.

Francis was no stickler for formalities, and for him the Pope's word was good enough. Overjoyed with their success, Francis and his brothers left Rome for their more familiar surroundings at Assisi. From this time on, they were all attached to the Church, and under its spiritual authority.

Hard Times
for the Brothers

On their return to Assisi, the first need of the brothers was for some kind of suitable shelter. They found it in a ruined and abandoned shed at a place called Rivo Torto, not far from the Portiuncula chapel. The shed was much too small to hold all of them with any comfort, and Francis had to dole out space sparingly. He resolved the problem by writing the name of each brother on the wall above the little area he was to occupy. The discomforts of the shed were, however, relatively minor. Much more difficult was the problem of getting bread.

Francis' Rule required all the brothers to work with their hands, and they regularly sought work in the fields and in the leper hospitals. All they were allowed to accept for their labor, however, was just enough food to subsist, and sometimes not even that was given them. When that happened, or when work was unavailable, they begged in town for scraps. Yet begging had its limitations, and the people of Assisi were not always generous. There were times when the brothers had to eat roots that they dug up in the fields.

Even when there was food, some brothers would suffer hunger through excessive fasting. Francis himself practiced fasting as a form of penance, but he didn't think it should be overdone. One night Francis was awakened by the moans of a brother who thought he was starving to death as the result of so much fasting. Francis immediately brought out whatever food there was and set the table. So that the hungry brother would not feel ashamed, Francis sat and ate with him. Afterwards he admonished all the brothers against excessive fasting. "My dear sons," he said, "everyone must consider his own nature. Some of you require more food than others to sustain life, and ought not to try to imitate those who need less. It is my desire that everyone shall give his body what it needs for being an efficient servant of the soul. For just as we must guard against eating too much food which injures body and soul alike, so must we guard against immoderate fasting. The Lord wants converts, not victims."

On another occasion, Brother Sylvester, the priest who had once complained that Francis had underpaid him for his stones, became ill. His illness was hardly noticed by the others — living so austerely, none of them looked very robust. Yet Francis did observe how feeble Sylvester seemed, and decided that what he needed was a good breakfast of grapes. Early one morning, when the other brothers were still sleeping, Francis awoke Sylvester and escorted him to a nearby vineyard. Then he picked a large cluster of grapes for Sylvester, and ate a few of them himself to spare Sylvester any feelings of shame or guilt. It was a simple act of kindness, but Sylvester was so touched by it that afterwards he could never recall the experience without tears brimming in his eyes.

Francis also forbade the brothers to inflict torture on themselves by wearing chains around their waists or other ascetic devices. Yet if Francis was tender and solicitous toward his brothers, he could be as tough as he had to be. When a newcomer to the Order turned out to be an idler who declined either to work or to beg for his food, Francis swiftly expelled him, saying, "Go your way, brother drone. You are good only at eating the honey gathered by the busy bees."

Similarly, Francis rejected a young man who wished to become a member of the Order but did not observe honestly the conditions for joining. Instead of giving all his possessions to the poor, he gave them to his family, which was not in any need. When he told Francis what he had done, Francis laughed and told him to go back to his family. "You have given your goods to your blood relations," he said, "and have cheated the poor. You are not worthy to be counted among God's poor yourself. Go your way."

During the months they spent at Rivo Torto, the brothers did not attempt any long missionary journeys. Yet the news that their Order had been recognized by the Pope had created a good deal of excitement in Assisi and its vicinity. Before long, Francis was invited to preach in the Church of San Giorgio. When the crowds that came to hear him became too big, he was offered the pulpit in the larger Cathedral of San Rufino. His sermons in these churches were not very different from those he had delivered in the streets. As always, he used simple language, avoiding flowery words or subtle phrases, and he spoke in Italian, which everyone understood. In keeping with his promise to Pope Innocent, he avoided questions of doctrine, and sought only to rekindle the flame of their old faith based upon the Gospel. He spoke invariably of the blessings of peace and love. He denounced the spirit of hatred and envy, and the lust for power, that brought conflict between classes and cities. Again and again he warned his listeners not to place their trust in riches, and urged them to give up wealth they had obtained dishonestly, or did not need.

Francis' preaching in Assisi seems to have touched the consciences of many people. Some, in fact, did distribute their wealth among the poor and turned to good works. Francis' preaching appears to have had a very dramatic effect in one other respect. The conflict between Assisi and Perugia that began in 1202, when Francis was taken prisoner, had never really been settled. It broke out again and again, each time more fiercely than before. The war had begun as a revolt of the *minores* — the "lesser" citizens — of Assisi against the *majores* — the "greater" citizens. The majores, the privileged nobility, had appealed to Perugia for help, provoking the conflict between the two cities. On November 9, 1210, the feuding parties within Assisi signed an agreement in which they pledged to work together in the future for the common good, and not to enter into any separate alliances with other cities, the Emperor, or the Pope. In other clauses, the nobility agreed to give up some of their feudal privileges, and amnesty was granted to all political exiles.

Francis might well have been overjoyed by this end to civil discord within Assisi. Love had triumphed over strife, and Assisi could prosper peacefully.

Soon after the agreement was signed, Francis chose a name for his Order. Until this time, the brothers had usually called themselves "Penitents from Assisi," but this name had no official status. Then one day, the Rule of the Order was being read aloud in Latin, and Francis was struck by a phrase in the following passage:

"Let the brethren, wherever they may find themselves called to labor or to serve, never take an office that shall put them over others but, on the contrary, *let them always be lower* than those who may be in that house."

The Latin word for "lower" or "lesser" — minores — seemed to Francis just the word to describe the humble condition and rank that he wished for his followers. Consequently he named his group the Order of Friars (brothers) Minor, so that all would know that they were, in the words of Thomas of Celano, "truly very little people."

The stay of the brothers at Rivo Torto ended in a rather unusual fashion. One day they were praying together in their shed when a peasant appeared with his donkey. Soon the peasant began pushing the donkey into the shed, saying, "Inside with you, long ears, we shall be most comfortable in this place." The peasant was apparently determined to take over the place for himself and his animal. Francis was deeply disturbed by the man's rudeness, but he made no effort to resist. Instead, he asked his brothers to leave the place, remarking with a touch of humor, "I know, brethren, that God has not called us to maintain a stable for asses, but to pray and show men the way of salvation!"

The Idyllic Years

The brothers were becoming more numerous, and it was clear to Francis that they now required a permanent home, preferably one near a chapel where they could pray undisturbed. Francis appealed first to Bishop Guido and the clergy of the Cathedral of San Rufino, but they were unable to help him. The problem was finally resolved by the abbot of the Benedictine monastery on Mount Subasio, where once Francis had worked in the kitchen. Both the Portiuncula chapel and the grounds around it were the property of the Benedictines, and the abbot offered them to Francis permanently. Francis was thrilled to receive the Portiuncula as a home for his Order, but he would not accept it as an outright gift. Instead, he insisted that he and his brothers would occupy it only as tenants, paying a token rent of one basket of fish a year. And each year, the abbot sent back a bottle of olive oil as a receipt.

The friars now began building quarters for themselves beside the Portiuncula chapel. Unlike the substantial, walled residences of some monastic Orders, these were extremely primitive. Each brother had a hut made of slender branches that were woven around poles, covered over with mud, and thatched with leaves. A larger cabin that served as a community house was built in similar fashion. Their "beds" consisted of some straw on the ground, and their pillows were small logs or even stones. They had no tables or chairs, but sat on the bare earth. The "walls" of their hermitage were nothing more than hedges. This was the way that Francis wanted all future residences for his brothers built. Even the churches, he said, "should be small and built of earth or wood."

The next few years at the Portiuncula were very possibly the happiest years of Francis' life, and the most idyllic time for his Order. Here in the woods around the chapel, Francis and his brothers strove to live in exact accordance with the Gospel, deriving happiness from the utter simplicity and humility of their existence. Such trials and suffering as they occasionally experienced they endured cheerfully and without complaining. Indeed, their Rule said, "Let the brothers refrain from murmuring. Let them not appear sad and gloomy like hypocrites, but let them show themselves joyous in the Lord, pleasant and cheerful, as is fitting." Francis would not tolerate a long face at the Portiuncula. Once when he saw one of the friars looking glum, he sent him back to his hut, saying, "If it is your sins that are troubling you, that is something between God and you. Go then, and ask His forgiveness, and then come back to us with a smiling face." Such instances of gloominess were rare, however, among the brothers in these days.

There was prayer and meditation at the Portiuncula, but there was work also, and Francis himself hired out as a common laborer. The friars worked chiefly in the hospitals for lepers, for these poor outcasts were especially dear to Francis. To him they were "God's patients," and deserved to be treated with reverence. Once a friar brought a leper, whose disease was far advanced, on a walk to the Portiuncula. Some of the brothers were distressed by this, and reproached him for it. The leper, of course, could hardly conceal his hurt feelings. Francis was deeply upset by the conduct of these brothers. He not only begged the leper's pardon, but as an example to the others, he shared a meal with the leper, eating out of the same bowl.

Though the brothers were obliged to work, Francis forbade them to accept money except in very rare cases, as when the sick were in dire need. He regarded money as a peculiarly unholy possession that had the effect of dehumanizing people. He saw all around him the arrogance and lust for power that money so often bred in those who had it. Grieved by the abuses that money brought, he wanted the utter poverty of his brothers to serve as a constant reproach to the greedy. And while he did not deny the right of others to own property, he always insisted that it was a trust put into their hands by the providence of God for the benefit of all who were in need.

Francis' aversion for money was so great, Brother Thomas tells us, that "he cursed it more than all other things and always said it was to be shunned as the devil himself." One day, a visitor to the Portiuncula left a coin upon the altar as an offering. A friar later saw the coin, picked it up, and put it on a window sill. Did he intend to use it eventually? We do not know, but Thomas tells us that Francis "rebuked him and upbraided him most severely because he had touched the money. He commanded him to lift the money from the window sill with his mouth and to place it with his mouth on the asses' dung heap outside the walls of the place. While that brother gladly fulfilled the command, fear filled the hearts of all who heard of it. All held in greater contempt for the future what was put on the level of dung."

On a later occasion, Peter of Catani told Francis that he could not possibly feed all those who were coming to visit the Portiuncula. Peter begged Francis to allow the Order to keep some of the goods of those entering it, so there would be some means to provide for the visitors. Francis rejected the idea as a violation of his Rule of poverty, however well-intentioned it was. "What would you have me do then?" asked Peter. "Strip the altar of the Blessed Virgin and sell its ornaments, since you cannot otherwise help the needy," Francis replied. "Believe me, she [Mary] would be more pleased to have the Gospel of her Son kept than that the altar should be ornamented and her Son despised."

Perhaps the most difficult lesson that Francis had to teach newcomers to his Order was to beg for their bread. Francis knew how trying it was for some of them, and always felt compassion for them. To encourage them, he would, as always, set an example by going out first himself to ask for alms. He was not upset when a newcomer confessed that he had felt ashamed to beg, but only when, because of shame, he would refuse to beg. In Francis' view, begging was an honorable exercise in humility. Even more, he felt it was a privilege, for Jesus himself had been a beggar.

One day, one of the shyer young brothers came back from begging door-to-door in Assisi with a bag of food slung over his shoulder. He was singing happily. Francis' joy was so great that he embraced the young friar and exclaimed, "Blessed be my brother who goes forth promptly, quests humbly, and comes back merrily."

The brothers begged, but they also gave alms as well. Their Rule clearly required it. "Let the brethren give to all who ask," it said. Frequently, all the brothers had to give were their tunics, so it is not surprising the number of times they parted with them when approached by beggars for alms. Francis appears to have outdone all the others in this respect, often to the distress of his disciples. "The brothers," one of Francis' biographers says, "had their work cut out for them in keeping the clothes on their master's back, especially because he would not wear new clothes, but always insisted on having those which had already been worn. Sometimes one brother would give half of his habit to Francis, and another the other half. Now and then the brothers tried to get back his clothes from those to whom he had given them, but Francis discovered this and therefore warned the beggar possessing them not to give them up without ample return."

In truth, Francis could not bear to see anyone poorer than himself or his brothers. He wished them to be the poorest of the poor, and when he would see a really ragged beggar on the road he would say, "We ought to be ashamed of ourselves. We want to be called poor and celebrated for our poverty, and here we see one who is much poorer than we, but does not boast of it." Then he would insist on giving all or part of his habit to the beggar, saying, "Let us give back to our brother Poor Man what we have borrowed from him."

At this time, approximately 1212–1215, the Order was growing rapidly. One reason for it was that Francis excluded almost no one from the Order who was willing to live according to the Gospel and to prove it by giving all his possessions to the poor. It did not matter whether he was of high birth or low, educated or unlettered, a sinner or not. If anything, Francis seems to have been partial to the downtrodden, and welcomed all those unfortunate and lost souls whom society normally casts out. His compassion extended even to criminals. One day three notorious robbers who had fallen on hard times came to a Franciscan hermitage to beg for bread. The friar who answered the door happened to be a former knight, and he was anything but hospitable to them. Denouncing them as thieves and murderers, he drove them away angrily.

Moments later Francis himself appeared at the hermitage carrying some bread and wine that he had begged. When he heard how the brother had turned away the robbers, he reproached him for his lack of charity. Then, according to one of the very early chronicles of Francis' life, he said, "I command you to take this loaf and this wine and go seek the robbers by hill and dale until you have found them, to offer them this as from me. Then kneel there before them and humbly ask their pardon. Then, but not until then, pray them in my name no longer to do wrong but to fear God. After that you may humbly return here."

The brother did as he was told, this biographer says, "while St. Francis on his part prayed God to convert the robbers. They returned with the brother, and when Francis gave them the assurance of the pardon of God, they changed their lives and entered the Order, in which they lived and died in a most holy manner."

Among the brothers who entered the Order in these early years were four who were destined to become his very close friends. Each one of them embodied one or more of the ideals that Francis esteemed so highly. Of all the members of his Order, Brother Leo was probably Francis' favorite. Because of his gentle, pure nature, Francis called him "Brother Little Lamb of God." Brother Leo was a priest, and Francis chose him to be both his confessor and secretary. In later years, when the Order was torn by dissension, Brother Leo was one of Francis' staunchest defenders.

Brother Masseo was a tall, fine-looking man who spoke eloquently. It is said that when he and Francis went begging together, Francis usually got only a few stale crumbs of bread, while Masseo was often given fresh, whole loaves. Francis apparently believed that Brother Masseo needed a lesson in humility. Consequently he assigned to Masseo the hardest and most menial jobs at the Portiuncula — cook, porter, and almsgiver. It was not until the other brothers interceded on Masseo's behalf that Francis relented. For a long time afterward, we are told, Brother Masseo prayed for the gift of humility, until it was finally granted. Because of Masseo's eloquence, Francis often took him with him on his missionary journeys.

Unlike Brother Masseo, Brother Rufino was timid and retiring, though he was of noble birth, and seems to have had a dread of preaching in public. He much preferred to live as a hermit in a cave, praying, as Francis said, "even in his sleep." One day, in an attempt to cure Brother Rufino of his shyness, Francis ordered him to go into Assisi and preach. Brother Rufino replied that he was a poor speaker and preferred to stay home. Francis then told him that, as a penance, he would have to preach without his tunic, wearing only his drawers.

Soon after Rufino left to do as he was ordered, Francis began to suffer remorse. Removing his own tunic, he set out for Assisi in his drawers. There he was ridiculed by the crowds, just as poor Rufino had been minutes before. Francis found Rufino preaching in church, trying desperately to make his voice heard above the laughter of the people. According to one of Francis' biographers, "Francis waited until the other had finished and then himself mounted the pulpit. He then preached so convincingly of the poverty and nakedness of Christ on the cross that the listeners all wept. As the two brothers left the church now clad in their habits [which Leo had brought them], the people crowded around to touch the hems of their garments."

Brother Juniper was noted for his almost child-like naiveté. Once, for example, a sick brother told Juniper how much he would like to eat some pig's feet. Juniper quickly grabbed a knife and ran into the woods where some pigs were foraging. In a moment, Juniper straddled the largest pig and cut off its foot, which he took back triumphantly to be cooked for the ailing brother. The owner of the pigs was quite furious, and complained to Francis bitterly. But Juniper so disarmed the man with his story of the brother's illness, and how much good the pig's foot had done him, that the owner finally butchered the pig and presented it to the brothers with his apologies. No wonder Francis used to say of Brother Juniper, "I wish I had a whole grove of such juniper trees!"

The qualities of gentleness, humility, and simplicity that so endeared these brothers to Francis existed to a large degree among practically all the friars in these early, idyllic times. Love, peace, and kindness prevailed at the Portiuncula. Perhaps not since the time of the Apostles had men striven so sincerely to realize Christ's ideals on earth, or come so close to succeeding.

Clare

When Francis was preaching at the Church of San Giorgio in Assisi, one of his listeners was a beautiful 16-year-old girl named Clare Scifi who came from a family of high nobility. Her father, Favorino, was a count, and one of those Assisian nobles who had appealed to Perugia for help when the citizens had become rebellious. Her home, a few steps from the Cathedral of San Rufino, was then the finest palace in the city. Clare's mother, Ortolana, was a pious woman who had made the long and dangerous pilgrimage to the Holy Land, as well as other journeys closer to home.

In the matter of piety, however, it soon became apparent that Clare would exceed even her. As a child, she prayed a great deal, keeping track of the actual number of prayers with pebbles, and liked to read about the lives of religious hermits. When she was 15, or possibly even younger, she had a most eligible suitor whom her parents decided she should accept. Clare not only rejected the suitor, but when pressed by her parents for a reason, told them that she was not interested in marriage and had decided to devote her life to God. This was more piety than either Favorino or Ortolana wished for, and they ceaselessly urged her to marry.

Like many other Assisians at this time, Clare was drawn to the sermons of the Little Poor Man, who was about 12 years older than herself. The story of his conversion, and the life of poverty that he had chosen, moved her deeply. She too wished to break away from the frivolousness of an idle and luxurious life and live like Francis in prayer, labor, and peace. Accompanied by a female cousin, she began visiting Francis secretly. He, in fact, had already heard about her from two friars who were also related to her, Sylvester and Rufino.

Clare told him how her parents were pressing her to marry, despite her own strong impulse to lead a religious life. He advised her not to yield to them, but to follow the calling she felt so keenly. In the following months, Francis became Clare's spiritual guide. Finally, when it was apparent that neither Clare nor her parents would change their views, it was decided that she should flee her home. Francis himself chose the date — the night of Palm Sunday, March 18, 1212. Clare was then 18.

That Sunday morning, Clare attended services at the Cathedral of San Rufino with her family, wearing her finest gown. This would be the last time she would ever pray with her mother and sisters in the church where she was baptized, the last day she would ever spend with them at home. She must have been overcome with emotion, for when the time came for the worshipers to go up to the altar rail to receive palm branches, she could not leave her pew. Bishop Guido saw her sitting alone with her head bowed, and very possibly understood; Francis may have confided his plans to him. In any event, he stepped down and brought to Clare the palm branch she had been unable to take herself.

It is possible too that Clare's parents also suspected what was afoot, for that night all the doors and windows of the Scifi palace were locked and barred. There was one exit, however, that had not occurred to them. In every Assisian house there was one door through which coffins were passed — the door of the dead. It was usually blocked up with stones or planks. Clare was able to clear away the stones and make her escape into the street. There she met her cousin and the two made their way in the dark to the Portiuncula. Then, as Clare knelt before the altar, Francis cut off her hair and covered her head with a tight black veil. In place of the silk dress she wore he gave her a coarse woolen robe belted by a rope, the same as the brothers wore, and a pair of wooden sandals. After Clare took the vows by which she became Sister Clare, Francis took her for asylum to a Benedictine convent two miles away.

It was a daring step for both Clare and Francis. He had no authority to accept women into his Order, or administer vows to them. He could have been censured by the Church, though he wasn't. As for Clare, she knew how angry her father would be, and that she would soon have to face his wrath by herself.

It didn't take Favorino long to find out where Clare had taken refuge. The next day he and his brothers went to the convent determined to bring her home. Clare received them in the chapel, listened to their pleas and promises, but would not budge. When it appeared that they might try to remove her by force, she clung to the altar, removed her veil, and showed them her shorn head. They withdrew then, but returned several times until Francis finally removed her to another Benedictine convent.

Only 16 days after Clare had left home, her younger sister, Agnes, joined her and received the veil from Francis. If Favorino had been angry before, he was furious now. He called upon his older brother, Monaldo, the head of the family, to bring Agnes back by any means necessary. Monaldo rode off to the convent with 12 armed men, terrorized the nuns, and then dragged Agnes kicking and screaming out of the convent. Hearing her cries for help, Clare prayed for divine intervention. According to legend, Agnes immediately became so heavy that she could not be dragged another inch. Then Clare came running onto the scene and commanded the abductors to leave. Instantly, the legend says, they became as meek as lambs and departed. In any event, they did not succeed in their mission, and later another Scifi sister, Beatrice, joined Clare and Agnes. After Favorino's death, Ortolana, their mother, also took the veil.

When Francis arranged for Clare to flee from her home, it is doubtful whether he had any intention of founding a second Order of nuns. In helping Clare, he was really acting in the best tradition of chivalry, which was so strong a part of his nature. Like a true knight, he was rescuing a damsel in distress and taking her under his protection. Yet just as his preaching in the streets of Assisi had led, without his planning it, to the development of the Friars Minor, so did his giving the veil to Clare lead inevitably to a second Order of sisters. Very soon, there were other women who wished to join Clare and Agnes, and it became apparent to Francis that he would have to find a suitable home for all of them who wished to follow his Rule of Gospel poverty.

Francis appealed to his old benefactors, the Benedictines of Mount Subasio, and they were generous again. This time, to Francis' great joy, they gave him San Damiano, whose chapel he had himself repaired, as a convent for the sisters. Soon after, Clare and a few other sisters moved in, and so the Order of Poor Ladies, or Poor Clares, was born.

Their Rule was very similar to that of the Friars Minor, especially in the matter of poverty, and Francis was their spiritual father. As always, Francis was chivalrous, and promised Clare, "For myself and for my Friars always to have for you as for them the same diligent care and special solicitude." Not only did Francis and the brothers minister to the Poor Ladies, but they shared with them the alms collected from begging.

During the early years of the two Orders, an informal relationship existed between them and it was not uncommon for the friars to visit the sisters or meet with them at the homes of friends. It was a potentially dangerous situation for two Orders pledged to chastity, and Francis was one of the first to perceive it. As a consequence, his own visits to San Damiano, which at first had been quite frequent, became more and more rare over the years. Yet his friendship with Clare herself remained ardent and steadfast until the very end of his life. He called her his "dear little spiritual plant," and she, in turn, revered him for the ideals with which he had inspired her.

Clare shared completely his devotion to poverty. Perhaps she was too hard on herself, for she fasted constantly, refused any food that was cooked, and slept on boards. Yet, like Francis, she counseled other members of her Order to be moderate in their asceticism. She shared too Francis' ideas about work. Despite her position as abbess, it was she who generally waited upon the sisters at mealtimes, and washed their feet when they returned from trips outside the convent. She cared for them when they were ill, and no task was too repugnant to her. Francis constantly sent sick people to her, and for a time San Damiano was something of a hospital.

Like Francis, she had a great deal of pluck, and fought hard for the ideals in which she believed, but especially for "the privilege of poverty." This privilege had been written into the Rule of the Poor Ladies that was approved by Pope Innocent III in 1215 or 1216. In fact, it is said that Innocent was so pleasantly surprised by this unusual request that he personally wrote into the Rule the first few lines of the paragraph authorizing poverty. In later years, however, it became the policy of the Papacy to ease the severe asceticism of both the Poor Clares and the Friars Minor, and to permit them to have property and revenues. Both Francis and Clare bitterly resisted the inroads that were made on the Rule of absolute poverty during their lifetimes.

In 1228, two years after Francis' death, Pope Gregory IX came to Assisi to attend the rites that made Francis a saint of the Church. Gregory personally visited Clare, whom he had known and admired a long time, and offered to release her from her vow of poverty so she could accept property for her convent. True to Francis' ideal she replied, "Holy Father, absolve me from my sins, but I have no desire for a dispensation from following our Lord Christ."

Gregory yielded to Clare on this occasion, but as early as 1219 convents of Poor Clares other than San Damiano had been permitted the right to own property and have regular incomes, and some had accepted. In 1247, Pope Innocent IV extended this right to *all* convents of Poor Ladies, but Clare never ceased to fight for her "privilege of poverty." Shortly before her death in 1253, she was visited by Pope Innocent IV. When Clare, who had been an invalid for a number of years, asked him to absolve her from her sins, he replied, "Would to God that I had as little need of it as you!"

Then Clare fought her last battle, imploring Innocent to restore "the privilege of most high poverty" to her Order. Her words were persuasive, and on August 10, 1253, she received his order permitting her and her sisters to live according to the Franciscan ideal. She died the next day, attended by some of Francis' dearest friends — Brothers Leo, Angelo, Juniper, and Giles, whose right to visit San Damiano she had always insisted upon, even in defiance of an earlier Papal prohibition against all visits by friars. Two years later, on August 15, 1255, Clare was made a saint of the Church.

The Lover of All Creation

At the time that Francis was founding the Order of Poor Ladies, he also undertook several missionary journeys throughout central and northern Italy. The reception given to him now was considerably different from what he and the brothers had encountered on their first missions. Almost everywhere Francis was hailed by the people as a living saint. His arrival in a town was often preceded by the ringing of church bells and people shouting, *"Ecco il santo!"* ("The saint is here!")

Such adulation embarrassed Francis, who was

quick to tell the crowds, "Do not make me a saint too soon, for I may yet bring sons and daughters into the world!" The more that people adored him and the friars for their poverty and humility, the more Francis seemed to feel the need to prove himself. On one occasion, for example, when he was ill, Francis ate some chicken. Apparently he felt great remorse about it, for as soon as he was well again he had a brother lead him through town at the end of a rope like a common criminal. All the while the brother shouted to the crowds, "Behold this great glutton who ate chicken without your knowing about it!"

Once Brother Masseo asked Francis why everyone ran to see and hear him, despite the fact that he was neither handsome, nor well educated, nor of noble birth. (Masseo was trying to test Francis' humility.) Francis' reply was, "Do you want me to tell you, Brother Masseo? Well, know that all this comes from God who, looking down and finding nothing viler on earth, quite naturally fixed his gaze on me. For to make his work shine forth in men's eyes, the Lord takes what is ignorant, weak, and despicable in preference to what is learned, strong, and noble, so that the creature may have no cause to glory, but the glory may go to the sole Author of all good."

As for bringing sons and daughters into the world, Francis *was* tempted by the idea of marriage and raising a family. How he handled this temptation on one occasion is related by Thomas of Celano. First, Francis whipped himself severely with his cord, saying, "Brother ass" — which is what he called his body — "this is what you deserve." But, Brother Thomas tells us, "when he saw that the temptation did not leave him even though all his body was marked with welts, he left his cell and cast himself naked into a deep pile of snow. Then, gathering handfuls of snow in the moonlight, he made seven lumps like human figures. Sitting before them, he began to speak, saying, 'Behold, this larger one is your wife. These four are your two sons and your two daughters. The other two are your servant and maid whom you must have to serve you. Hurry and clothe them all, for they are dying of cold. But if caring for so many of them troubles you, then serve God alone and don't think of anything else.'"

It was while Francis was making these triumphant missionary journeys that he delivered his celebrated sermon to the birds. It was an extraordinary sermon, the more so because Francis' time was only so recently removed from the Dark Ages, when men felt little sympathy either for nature or animals. Francis' love extended to all creation. From the sun to the lowliest earthworm, he saw everything in nature as part of God's work. No one felt, or expressed, as much as he the kinship that exists between men, animals, plants, the sea, and the stars. "Praised be Thou, Lord," he would pray, "with all Thy creatures, especially for my Brother Sun which gives us the day and by him Thou showest Thy light."

One day, near the town of Bevagna, Francis

saw a large flock of birds in a field. Moved by the sight, he left his companions and entered the field to preach to the birds.

"My little sisters," he said to them, "you ought to praise and love your Creator very much. For He has made you free to fly wherever you wish, and has given you the beautiful plumage that you wear. Praise Him too for the food He provides you without your having to sow or reap, for the beautiful voices He has given you, for your numbers that He has multiplied, and for the realm of pure air He has reserved for you. He gives you fountains and streams to drink from, mountains and hills in which to take refuge, and tall trees in which to build your nests. Although you do not know how to sew or spin, He gives you and your little ones the clothing you need.

"How the Creator must love you to grant you such favors! So my sister birds, do not be ungrateful, but continually praise Him who showers blessings on you."

Francis' love of birds and animals appears to have been returned in kind. There are innumerable stories that attest to the affection that they instinctively felt for him. The most famous of these is the legend of the wolf of Gubbio, a ferocious animal that was destroying a considerable amount of livestock in the area. Francis confronted his "brother wolf," scolded him, and then suggested a peace pact. The terms were these: If the wolf would stop killing other creatures, Francis would see to it that the people of Gubbio would feed him as long as he lived.

Both the wolf and the townspeople agreed to those terms, and thereafter the wolf became completely docile. When it finally died of old age, the people wept, for the sight of it trotting peacefully around the town had always reminded them of St. Francis. One of Francis' biographers suggests that this story might well be an allegory of how Francis restored peace between the citizens of a town and its savage, feudal overlord.

Francis was completely uninhibited in his feelings for animals. Once, for example, he bought some caged turtledoves and said to them, "Little sisters, you are simple, innocent, and chaste. Why did you let yourselves be caught? I shall save you from death, and have nests made for you, so that you may bring forth young and multiply according to the commandment of our Creator."

Then he made nests for them all, and the turtledoves began to lay eggs and bring up their broods, to the delight of the brothers.

Of all the birds, his favorite was the crested lark. "Sister lark with her little hood," he would tell the friars, "looks a little like us, and with her earth-colored plumage she urges us to be satisfied with our poor and coarse habits. She is humble enough to seek her food in dust and dung. Soaring high and praising the Lord with her song, she teaches us to despise earthly things and to make our dwelling even now in Heaven."

Francis, the lover of perfect poverty, permitted only one luxury at the Portiuncula. In fact, he commanded it. He admonished the brother who tended the garden to plant sweet-smelling flowers, and not just vegetables. And to these flowers, as well as the flowers in the fields, he talked also.

Francis' missionary journeys at this time were not confined to Italy. His was the age of Crusades, when Christian armies were fighting against the Moslems in the Holy Land, North Africa, and in Spain. In 1212, Francis himself was seized by the crusading fervor and asked Pope Innocent III's blessing for a mission to Syria. His aim was nothing less than to preach to the Saracens and convert them to Christianity. What other Christians had failed to accomplish by force of arms, he hoped to accomplish by peaceful persuasion. Was it an impossible dream? Perhaps. But his great success in preaching the Gospel in Italy may have led him to believe that nothing was impossible, and that Saracens too might be converted. Perhaps Francis was also drawn by the idea of shedding his own blood and becoming a martyr. Thomas of Celano tells us that Francis "was aflame with the utmost desire for martyrdom, and determined to pass over to Syria to preach the Christian faith and repentance to the Saracens."

In any event, Francis did obtain Innocent's blessing for a voyage to Syria, and he embarked sometime toward the end of 1212. His ship, however, was blown ashore on the Dalmatian coast (present-day Yugoslavia) during a storm. As winter was approaching, he had no alternative but to return to Italy. Without any money,

Francis and his traveling companion appear to have become stowaways. They more than compensated the ship's crew, whose rations were poor, by later sharing with them their ample supplies of food.

About two years later, in 1214, Francis attempted another journey to preach to the infidels. This time, his objective was Morocco, North Africa, where he hoped to convert the Sultan Mohammed ben Nasser. Not much is known about how Francis traveled this time. His early biographers tell us only that in his haste to reach the Sultan, he frequently outdistanced his companion, Bernard of Quintavelle, when they walked. In Spain, however, Francis became quite ill and again he had to return to Italy. It is quite possible that he made the return trip by way of France.

While precise information is often lacking about this period of Francis' life, one fact is quite certain. In the spring of 1213, after Francis' return to Italy from Dalmatia, he and a companion were in the province of Romagna. There they came upon the castle of Montefeltro, high on a hill. A relative of the lord of the castle had just been knighted, and a celebration was taking place. The gayety of the festivities did not deter Francis and his companion from entering the courtyard of the castle where all the local nobility were assembled. Neither was Francis deterred from preaching by the wealth and splendor of the gathering. He took for his theme a couplet from a poem of chivalry:

I aspire to so great a treasure
That all pain for me is pleasure.

Francis then described the suffering that the Apostles had endured to achieve an eternal reward. Many of the knights and ladies were deeply moved. One of them, Count Orlando of Tuscany, afterward told Francis that he owned a mountain, La Verna, that was quite isolated and ideally suited for solitary prayer and meditation. "If it pleased you," he said, "I would willingly give it to you and your brothers for the salvation of my soul."

Francis accepted the gift joyfully, and an authentic deed confirms the fact that Mount La Verna was given to the brothers on May 8, 1213. At a later date, La Verna would be the scene of perhaps the most significant event in Francis' life.

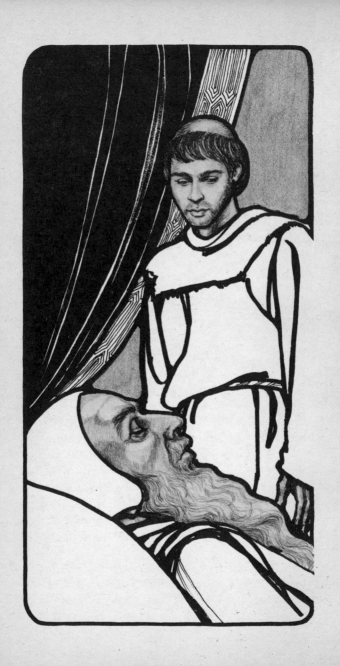

The Nonviolent Reformer

n the year 1215, Pope Innocent III summoned to Rome a large gathering of religious leaders from all of Europe and the Near East, plus the representatives of all Christian ruling sovereigns. It is generally believed that Francis attended this meeting, called the Fourth Lateran Council, and without doubt it was of great significance both to himself and his Order.

Pope Innocent told the great assemblage that he had called it together for two reasons, to bring about a reform of the Church, and to launch a new crusade to wrest the Holy Land from the Saracens. The two objectives were not unrelated. A new crusade would inevitably create a religious fervor conducive to reform which, Innocent believed, was essential to combat the heresies then threatening the Church.

The Pope deplored the scandals that were bringing dishonor upon the Church and called on the Council to "smite without pity" those clerics guilty of greed and ambition. Then he engaged in some symbolism. He told the Council to spare only those clerics marked by the Greek letter Tau, or T. The letter Tau, he explained, "has exactly the same form as the Cross on which our Lord was crucified. And," he concluded, "only those [clergymen] will be marked with this sign and will obtain mercy who have conformed their life to that of the Crucified Savior." What the Pope meant was that the Council should expel from the Church those clergymen tainted by corruption and retain only those who were truly devoted to the religious life.

Francis was deeply impressed by these words of the Pope. They seemed to him a confirmation of his own ideal of the religious life and of his mission as an apostle. From then on, Francis made the letter Tau, the symbol of reform, the emblem of his Order. He used it as a signature, placed it on his writings, and even painted it on his door.

If Francis took Innocent's words almost as a personal message, he may have been justified. For among its decisions, the Lateran Council officially approved Francis' Rule, which Innocent had only tentatively approved six years earlier. It also recognized another new monastic Order noted for its missionary zeal, the Dominicans. Its founder, Dominic de Guzman, a Spanish cleric, was also destined to become a saint. The recognition of these two Orders at this time was not a coincidence. Rather it was evidence that the Church intended to utilize them from this time on as the chief forces with which to regenerate the clergy and overcome heresy.

Ironically, Innocent III died within a few months after setting these forces in motion. Francis was at his deathbed in Perugia, paying final homage to the great pontiff who had approved his work. By contrast, most members of the Curia were absent, busy with their own affairs. We get a first-hand account of the scene at Perugia from Jacques de Vitry, a French clergyman who had traveled there to be consecrated as a bishop. He arrived on July 16, 1216, and learned that Innocent had died that very morning. In a letter to his friends at home, he gives his impression of the Curia:

"The members are so taken up by political affairs and by lawsuits and so preoccupied by everything having to do with kings and states that it is hardly possible to get in a word about religious matters. All this caused me much grief."

Then de Vitry describes the Franciscans whom he met on his travels in northern Italy:

"The thing that has consoled me is the sight of so many men and women who have aban-

doned their wealth and forsaken the world for
the love of Christ. These men, who bear the
name of Friars Minor, are held in the highest
esteem by the Pope and cardinals. Utterly un-
interested in temporal concerns, they devote all
their efforts to drawing souls away from the
vanities of the world. By the grace of God, they
have already achieved great success and made
numerous converts. As for their mode of life,
it is that of the primitive Church. They have no
churches, no residences, no fields, nor vineyards,
nor animals, nor houses, nor property where
they can harbor their heads. During the day they
are to be found in the cities and villages, preach--
ing or working. At night they return to their
hermitages or retire to a solitary spot to pray.

"The women dwell together in refuges near
the cities, living by the work of their hands
without accepting any gifts. They are so humble
that they grieve much that they are honored
more than they wish by clergy and laity alike."

It is the golden age of the Franciscans — the
Friars Minor and the Poor Ladies working with
their hands, shunning all honors, happy in their
devotion.

Innocent III was succeeded within two days of
his death by Honorius III. To hasten the election,
an early biographer reports, "the Perugians had
decided to lock up the members of the Curia and
to progressively decrease their rations."

Honorius was quite old and in poor health, yet
he appears to have impressed Jacques de Vitry
favorably: "An excellent and pious old man has
just been elected Pope," he wrote, "and he is

furthermore a plain and benevolent man who has given almost all his fortune to the poor."

Under Honorius, the relationship between the Papacy and the Friars Minor began to grow much closer. More than Honorius himself, the man responsible for bringing about this close relationship was Cardinal Ugolino, the most influential member of the Curia for many years, who later became Pope Gregory IX. From about this time, Cardinal Ugolino would take Francis under his wing, become the official protector of the Friars Minor, and guide the Order during the very stormy period that lay ahead.

A relative of Pope Innocent III, Ugolino was by all accounts a handsome and learned man of great energy and skill. He was likewise a pious man who had a special fondness for monastics, in whom he saw the greatest hope for reforming the Church. His affection for both Francis and Clare was very great, and he expressed it in many touching ways. Yet he was also a practical man of affairs, and while he venerated Francis for his holiness, he did not believe that all of Francis' ideas were capable of realization. In general, he sought to accommodate Francis' ideal to whatever he considered to be the best interest of the Church, as well as the friars themselves. More often than not, this meant easing the Rule of absolute poverty to permit both the friars and the Poor Ladies a more comfortable and practical existence. Though he tried very hard to spare Francis pain, it was inevitable that Il Poverello would suffer anguish at seeing his ideal of Gospel poverty compromised.

We get some glimpse of Cardinal Ugolino's practical turn of mind in two of his earliest suggestions for the Friars Minor. On one occasion, Dominic, inspired by Ugolino, proposed to Francis a merger of their two Orders. For Ugolino, such a union would have obvious administrative advantages. Perhaps too he already had some misgivings about what he considered Francis' shortcomings as an organizer. Francis declined Dominic's offer to unite their Orders, but not his request for a souvenir of their meeting — the rope that Francis wore around his waist.

Sometime later, Cardinal Ugolino proposed to Dominic and Francis that recruits to the ranks of the higher clergy should be chosen from among their friars. Here Ugolino was motivated chiefly by his interest in Church reform. Both Dominic and Francis declined this proposal, but Francis' reply was particularly firm:

"Your Lordship," he said, "my brothers are called *fratres minores* [Friars Minor] that they may not attempt to become *majores* [majors]. Their vocation teaches them ever to remain in an humble condition. Keep them in it, even against their will, if you would have them be useful to the Church. And never, I beg of you, permit them to become prelates."

Francis' close personal relationship with Cardinal Ugolino began in 1217, although Ugolino had already interested himself in the Friars Minor before that. In the meantime, Francis had some important business with the newly elected Pope, Honorius III. Accompanied by Brother Masseo, Francis visited the Pope at Perugia only

a few weeks after his election. He startled
Honorius by asking for an extraordinary privilege, one intended primarily to help the poor. It
was that all those who would come to the Portiuncula chapel in the future to confess their sins
and receive absolution from a priest should be
released from all guilt and punishment for sins
"from the day of their baptism to the day they
entered the chapel."

Such a sweeping indulgence, or pardon for
sins, for ordinary churchgoers was quite unheard
of. It *was* granted to those who joined the ranks
of the Crusaders to the Holy Land. Later this
privilege was extended to others, particularly
those who made long pilgrimages or, sometimes,
made donations for the repair of churches. But
Francis wanted this privilege not just for those
who could go crusading, or make long journeys,
or contribute large sums of money. He wanted it
for all the poor people who could visit the Portiuncula and would not have to make any dona-
tion. Honorius protested that the Curia did not
grant such a broad indulgence to any church, but
Francis insisted that the Lord himself had sent
him on this mission. When Honorius appeared to
yield, several cardinals objected strongly. They
said that such a privilege would cheapen the
value of pardons granted for crusading or pilgrimages to Rome. Finally Honorius resolved the
problem by restricting the indulgence to one day
each year. The day fixed upon was August 2, the
date on which the restored chapel was to be
consecrated.

Francis started to depart but was called back

by the Pope. "So you are leaving, simple little man," Honorius said, "without any document proving that this indulgence has been granted?" Francis replied, "Holy Father, your word is enough for me. If this indulgence is the work of God, it will be made manifest."

Francis and Masseo then returned to the Portiuncula. On August 2, Francis told the gathering there, "I want to send you all to Paradise, and I have received for you an indulgence from the Holy Father. All you who have come here today, and all who shall come yearly on this day, shall have an indulgence for all your sins." Then he added rather ingenuously, "I wanted it for one week, but I could get it for only one day."

Missions to Foreign Lands

ike King Arthur who summoned the Knights of the Round Table together each year at Pentecost, Francis decided about 1216 to hold regular meetings of the Friars Minor at the Portiuncula on the same occasion. These meetings, or chapters, were designed to reunite Francis with old friends, many of whom were now living in hermitages elsewhere, and to give him the opportunity of meeting many new friars. At these early chapters, Francis would preach to the brothers and imbue them with his ideals.

"We Friars Minor," he would tell them, "what are we other than God's singers and players who seek to draw hearts upwards and to fill them with spiritual joy?"

They were, in effect, troubadours whose mission was to sing of the beauty and joy of serving the Lord. Francis himself had done this in Assisi. Now he assigned this role to all the brothers.

Because the friars owned virtually nothing but the clothes on their backs, there was at first very little in the way of "official business" to attend to. As a consequence, these first chapters had a carefree quality that was enhanced by their bucolic, outdoor setting. As usual, the brothers slept in their reed and mud huts or under the trees, lying on the bare ground or on straw.

The first chapter of the friars held in 1216 was attended by Cardinal Ugolino. He came to the Portiuncula on horseback, dressed in his princely robes, accompanied by a brilliant escort of nobles and clerics, including Dominic and some of his friars. At the sight of the Friars Minor who came to greet him — about 5,000 of them — Ugolino was moved to tears and exclaimed, "Here is the army of Christ's knights all ready for battle!" Then he dismounted, removed his cloak and shoes, and walked barefoot to the chapel to say Mass. Francis preached the sermon, taking as his subject a line of verse, "Suffering is light, but the glory to come is infinite."

Later Cardinal Ugolino inspected the primitive huts of the friars. When he saw how poorly they lived, he was again overcome by emotion and cried out, "How will it go with us who live so luxuriously day after day in superfluity and delights?"

Dominic too was amazed by the asceticism of the Franciscans, and wondered how all the brothers at the chapter would be fed. For Francis certainly had made no plans to feed such a large gathering, as usual placing his trust in God. The providential answer soon came. From all over the countryside, a seemingly endless procession of peasants descended on the Portiuncula with donkeys laden with food and wine for the friars. They brought far more than was actually needed, and even supplied all the necessary plates and glasses. Dominic was so impressed by the devotion of the people to the Friars Minor that he vowed on the spot to make Gospel poverty the rule for his Order too.

Because Francis' Order was growing so rapidly, the Chapter of 1217 had to take up the problem of organization. It was decided to divide the Brotherhood into regional provinces, with a "minister" at the head of each. Subdivisions were headed by "custodians," while residences were headed by "guardians." Francis expressly chose those names because none of them suggested the idea of authority or importance. He wished above all to preserve the spirit of near equality in his Order. In defining the role of these new superiors, Francis said, "They ought to be the servants of the other friars, visit them frequently, instruct, encourage, and watch over them, like a shepherd over his sheep. . . . And in their actions, let all be inspired by the holy Gospel, which commands us not to do to others what we would not wish done to us."

The Chapter of 1217 also decided to send missions outside Italy for the first time to establish the Order in other countries. These missions were fraught with danger, and Francis, before calling for volunteers, warned them accordingly. The experiences of the first missions in Italy were still fresh in his mind. How might foreigners react to the brothers who did not know their language, had no letters of introduction from Church authorities, and no money? Francis himself would not permit the brothers to have letters of introduction. After all, Christ's Apostles carried no credentials. Why should the Friars Minor?

As always, Francis set the example, electing to go to France. He told the brothers that the French were especially dear to him because of their strong reverence for the sacrament of Communion, which he himself greatly loved. It is possible too that he was drawn to France because it was the country to which he owed his name, the chivalrous dreams of his youth, and all the poetry and songs that had so charmed him.

After advising the other volunteers to travel by two's and to be humble and gentle wherever they went, Francis set out on his own mission accompanied by Brother Pacifico. He planned to reach France by crossing the Alps. Arriving in Florence, he looked up Cardinal Ugolino who was there to preach the new Crusade. Francis was greatly surprised when Ugolino urged him strongly to call off his mission to France. "You must not cross the mountains," Cardinal Ugolino said, "when there are still so many prelates in the Curia who look with disfavor on your Order and wish nothing better than to stir up difficulties for you. There are cardinals like myself who are favorably disposed to your Order, but we cannot help you if you leave at this time."

Francis protested that he would feel ashamed to stay at home while the other friars were taking risks in foreign lands. When Ugolino admonished him for sending them on such dangerous missions, Francis replied, "My Lord, God wants my friars to spread out over the whole world. It is their vocation to win souls, not only in Christian lands, but even among the infidels whom they shall convert."

Ugolino could not quarrel with the missionary vocation of the friars, but he did persuade Francis to remain in Italy.

What were the dangers that faced Francis in the Curia? Undoubtedly some cardinals were jealous of his success, and rankled by the indulgence he had won for the Portiuncula. Others still suspected Francis and his brothers of being heretics because of their unorthodox way of living. To some, Francis was a dangerous visionary. To defend Francis, and to develop his own plans for the Order, Cardinal Ugolino needed Francis at home.

As for the brothers who traveled abroad, they generally fared quite badly. They were usually taken for heretics, and without any credentials or the ability to make themselves understood, they had a hard time proving they were not.

They often suffered the most cruel and abusive treatment as a result. In Hungary, for example, they were taken for religious quacks and driven from the cities. In the countryside, the farmers set their dogs on them. In Germany, where they were suspected of being heretics, they were treated even worse. There the brothers were arrested, bound naked to the pillory, and whipped until they bled. They went home as soon as possible and told the friars of their ordeal. Some of the friars were so affected that they added to their prayers, "Lord preserve us from heresy and the ferocity of the Germans."

It was about this time, 1218, that the first signs of dissension began to appear in Francis' Order. In the early years, Francis' followers had venerated him as a father and an infallible prophet. Francis and his closest disciples had hand-picked the new recruits to the Order, and these brothers were loyal to Il Poverello's ideal. But when the Order began to expand so rapidly many men entered it who hardly knew Francis at all, and they soon outnumbered the early followers. Many of these new recruits found apostolic poverty hard to take. They preferred to live more comfortably, like the monastics of other Orders that owned large estates and had impressive living quarters. Also, some of these new recruits were educated men who tended to look down on Francis as "unlettered," and perhaps even anti-intellectual. Francis, in fact, forbade the brothers to have books, not only because books were property, but because he believed that too much book-learning was incompatible with his ideals of complete simplicity and humility. Too much book-learning made some men proud, and there was no room for false pride in the Friars Minor. As far as Francis was concerned, the only learning a brother really required was to be found in the Gospel, and he looked with disfavor, if not suspicion, on other books. Among the more learned recruits there was also a desire to follow the Rules of older Orders whose monks were permitted to devote themselves to study.

Some indications of things to come took place at the chapter of 1219. Shortly before the meeting, while Francis was away, a stone building was constructed alongside the Portiuncula chapel. It was built by the town of Assisi, with the approval of the dissident friars, to provide the brothers with better accommodations for their meetings. When Francis returned and saw the stone building, he was beside himself with anger. It was, he felt, a mockery of holy poverty. He quickly clambered up to the roof and, aided by some of his loyal followers, began to dismantle it tile by tile. He would have torn down the whole building, but he was told that it belonged to the town of Assisi, and he rather regretfully stopped.

An even more painful experience awaited him at this chapter. Some of the more learned, dissident friars appealed to Cardinal Ugolino, who was at the meeting, to intervene with Francis on their behalf. Specifically, they wanted Francis to consult and be guided by them, and to give them greater responsibilities in the affairs of the Order. They also wanted him to consider revising his Rule to make it conform more with those of the older Orders. Ugolino conveyed their wishes to Francis as diplomatically as possible, but Francis was deeply upset. He made no reply to Ugolino but, taking him by the hand, he went to address the meeting.

"My brothers," he said with great emotion, "the Lord has called me into the ways of simplicity and humility. And He has shown me that this is the true way for myself and for all those who would trust in me and choose to follow me. So do not speak to me of the Rule of St. Benedict, or St. Augustine, or St. Bernard, or any other Rule except that which God has most mercifully chosen to give me. The Lord said to me that He wished me to be a simple fool in this world, but you with all your wisdom and learning will be damned by Him. God will punish you and, whether you like it or not, will force you to return to your vocation!"

The vehemence with which Francis uttered these words completely intimidated the rebellious friars and astonished Cardinal Ugolino. No more was said at this meeting about changing Francis' Rule.

The meeting did decide to send more missions to Christian lands and, bolder yet, to Moslem countries too. Francis himself chose to go to Egypt where crusading armies were besieging the city of Damietta. This time, Ugolino raised no objections. After appointing two vicars to take charge of the Order in his absence, Francis embarked for the Holy Land on June 24, 1219, accompanied by a few other friars. They reached

Damietta, at the mouth of the Nile, about a month later, after first landing at Acre. What Francis saw of the crusaders at Damietta disillusioned him greatly. While some of them were unquestionably men of zeal, many others were simply adventurers, interested mainly in plunder and debauchery. On August 29, this demoralized army launched a heavy attack on Damietta and suffered a disastrous defeat, losing more than 4,000 men. Francis had predicted that the attack would fail and now he was hailed as a prophet. For a time, at least, his preaching appears to have improved the moral climate among the crusaders, and he received a number of them into his Order. Jacques de Vitry was at Damietta and wrote that "Francis is so lovable that he is venerated by everyone."

Francis, however, was not satisfied to save souls among the Christian crusaders. It was always his dream to convert the Saracens, and one day he set out toward the enemy lines accompanied by a brother, Illuminato. It was an act of enormous courage, for in those days Moslems and Christians gave little quarter. A Christian head, in fact, fetched a handsome reward in the Sultan's camp. Francis sang as he approached the Saracen outposts, and comforted Illuminato with advice to "put your trust in Him who sends us forth like sheep in the midst of wolves."

The two were soon seized by Saracen guards who proceeded to rough them up. But Francis kept shouting, "Soldan! Soldan!" ("Sultan! Sultan!") at the top of his lungs and somehow conveyed the impression that he and Illuminato were peace envoys. The guards clapped them in chains and eventually they were brought before the Moslem Sultan, Melek El-Kamil. Francis informed the Sultan in French that he had come to convert him to the true faith, which ordinarily was a fairly sure way to lose one's head. Fortunately, El-Kamil was a tolerant and quite chivalrous man himself, and he rather admired Francis' pluck. In fact, he invited Francis to stay with him a few days. According to some accounts, Francis offered to prove the superiority of his religion by walking unharmed through a curtain of fire. Would the Sultan then be willing to acknowledge Christ as the true Savior? The Sultan replied that he could not do so without alienating his people, and all other attempts at persuasion were also unavailing. El-Kamil offered his guest numerous gifts, but Francis accepted only one. It was a small horn that he later used to summon people when he preached. It can still be seen in Assisi today among his other relics.

When Francis finally departed, understandably feeling quite disappointed, El-Kamil said to him, "Pray that God may reveal to me that faith which is most pleasing to Him." Then he sent Francis and Illuminato back to the Christian lines escorted by a guard of honor.

Not all of Francis' brothers who ventured into Moslem lands were so fortunate. In Morocco, five of the brothers persistently preached that Mohammed was a false prophet, even entering mosques in their zeal. The exasperated authorities made several attempts to deport the brothers unharmed, but each time they returned. They finally achieved the martyrdom they so earnestly sought when they were beheaded after bravely enduring the most terrible tortures. The news of their martyrdom reached Francis months later. According to some accounts, he is reported to have exclaimed, "Now I can truly say that I have five real Brothers." Other accounts say that he admonished the other friars not to take undue pride in their deaths, remarking, "Let everyone exult in his own martyrdom and not in that of others."

Damietta finally fell to the crusaders in November 1219. Francis was appalled by what he saw — the streets filled with corpses, and the crusaders savagely fighting among themselves over the vast booty. He left as soon as he could, taking a ship for Acre. He spent the next several months visiting the shrines of the Holy Land, which was then partly Christian and partly Moslem. He was aided by a permit granted him by the Sultan of Damascus, a brother of El-Kamil. Then one day in the summer of 1220 a brother arrived from the Portiuncula with very bad news. The vicars whom Francis had left in charge of the Order back home were destroying all his work, and he implored Francis to return at once. With three other brothers, Peter of Catani, Elias, and Caesar of Speyer, Francis embarked immediately for Italy to try to save his Order.

The Crisis
in Francis' Order

What had taken place in the Order during Francis' one-year stay in the Near East? The two brothers whom Francis had appointed vicars when he left, Matthew of Narni and Gregory of Naples, had proved to be most unfortunate choices for him and his loyal followers. They belonged completely to the faction of friars that found Francis' Rule too hard, or too narrow. They had taken advantage of Francis' absence to put through new regulations that were completely contrary to Francis' ideals. In general, their aim was to alleviate the vow of poverty, tighten up discipline, and multiply the number of fasts and penances. Perhaps these last measures — increased fasting and privation — may appear to be in keeping with Francis' ideal of poverty and self-denial. In truth, they were quite contradictory. Francis did not view the apostolic life as a somber, painful experience. He defined "perfect joy" as the ability to withstand adversity with patience and humility, but this had nothing to do with such formalities as the number of times one fasted a week, or how many penances one did. He had admonished the brothers against excessive fasting and wearing somber faces, which he regarded as false piety. He believed too that needless fasting was contrary to the Gospel, for Jesus had told his apostles, "And whatever town you enter, and they receive you, *eat what is set before you.*" Francis had made this a part of his Rule, granting the brothers permission "to eat of whatever foods are put before them."

Francis was incensed by the new regulations that increased fasting, as well as the use of large and imposing buildings by some of the friars in his absence. He got his first glimpse of one of these when he arrived in Bologna on his return from the Near East. It was not only a residence for the friars, but a school as well, and contrary to all his ideas, the friars considered it their property. One can well imagine Francis' rage at the sight of this great house *owned* by the friars and used to advance book-learning! He summoned its minister, Peter Staccia, before him and gave him a tongue-lashing. "Are you trying to destroy my Order," he asked, "forgetting that it is my will that the friars spend less time in study than in prayer?" Then he cursed Staccia and ordered everyone, including the sick, to vacate the building at once. (Later Cardinal Ugolino persuaded Francis to reopen the school, which he deemed essential for a preaching Order. Ugolino convinced Francis that the school and books were actually Papal property and that he, Ugolino, was merely letting the friars use it.)

Francis was angered too because the vicars had requested and received Papal letters of introduction for the brothers going out on missionary journeys. He once said that he wanted no privileges from the Papacy except the privilege to have none. The only exception to this rule, the indulgence he had asked for the Portiuncula, was for the benefit of the poor who would get their reward in Heaven. Francis saw his Rule crumbling all about him. In his absence, Cardinal Ugolino had granted convents of Poor Ladies other than San Damiano permission to live under a Rule that allowed them to own property. Some had accepted it.

The efforts to tighten discipline within the Order were probably warranted. The success of the Order, its great growth in numbers, had become one of its greatest problems. Francis' Rule consisted basically of a few brief sentences from the Gospel — "Sell all you have," "Take up your cross," "Take nothing with you for your journey," and so forth. Except for these simple Gospel admonitions, there were few formal rules for the brothers' conduct. In fact, they enjoyed a great deal of freedom, some living as hermits, others as day laborers or nurses, and still others as pilgrims and wandering preachers. When the Order was small and Francis could control it personally, there were few problems. But when it numbered thousands and got beyond his personal control, there were bound to be difficulties. Some of the brothers were living as vagabonds. Some had rather strange ideas — one wanted to found a new Order composed of lepers of both sexes.

Faced with a revolt on the part of those brothers who found his Rule too hard, and disorders on the part of those for whom it was perhaps too easy, Francis began to feel his Order slipping away from him. One night he had a dream in which he saw a mother hen unable to shelter all her chicks under her wing. The dream, of course, expressed Francis' growing concern about his inability to control his Order. Sensing his own helplessness, he decided to ask Pope Honorius for an official protector to oversee his Order, and specifically requested Cardinal Ugolino. Honorius granted his wish, and from then on Ugolino became the "protector, governor, and corrector of the Brotherhood," and Francis' permanent advisor. Undoubtedly Ugolino saw himself as a kind of arbiter between the two rival factions in Francis' Order, those who wished to follow Francis' ideal, and those who thought it too impractical. If Ugolino's decisions generally favored the latter, it would be hard to accuse him, as some have, of bad faith toward Il Poverello and of "turning his Order to the profit of the Church." Basically Ugolino believed that Francis' ideal could be realized only by a few very exceptional souls, such as Brother Leo and Brother Giles, but for the great majority they were Utopian. Now that there were so many friars, he felt they needed permanent homes, schools, and an assured income. Though he did, in fact, mitigate the rule of poverty, he preserved much of the Franciscan spirit, and defended the Order against those who would have condemned it as heretic.

Many of Francis' loyal followers had revolted against the new regulations of the vicars, and had been persecuted severely as a result. Their lot was not helped by the fact that Francis, because of his long absence, was believed to be dead. A number of them fled to escape persecution. It was one of these brothers who found Francis in the Holy Land and urged him to return home.

Francis now had a protector and advisor in Cardinal Ugolino, and various decisions were soon reached in an effort to restore harmony within the Order. The two rebellious vicars, who had the support of some members of the Curia, were dismissed. The would-be Order of lepers was dissolved, and steps were taken to curtail vagabondage. To weed out undesirables in the future, a one-year novitiate, or trial period, was required of all new recruits. Finally, Ugolino commissioned Francis to write a new Rule for the Order, one that would be a more formal document than his first Rule. This was to be ready in time for the chapter of 1221.

Despite these steps, Francis continued to be filled with self-doubts. Perhaps he understood that his Order now required a businesslike administrator to head it and enforce discipline, and he realized his own shortcomings for such a role. "I am not an executioner," he used to say. He decided, therefore, to resign as the titular head of the Order at the Chapter of 1220, and to turn it over to Peter of Catani, who was a lawyer. Some idea of the terrible anguish that this must have caused him can be gathered from the following account of his resignation speech to the friars:

" 'From now on,' he told the friars, 'I am dead for you, but here is Brother Peter of Catani whom you and I will all obey.' And prostrating himself before Peter he promised him obedience and submission. The friars could not restrain their tears and lamentations when they saw themselves thus becoming orphans of a sort. But Francis arose and, clasping his hands, with eyes raised to heaven, said, 'Lord, I return to you this family that you have confided to me. Now I have no longer strength nor ability to keep on caring for them. I confide them, therefore, to the ministers. May they be responsible before you, Lord, at the day of judgment if any brother, by their negligence or bad example, or by a too severe discipline, should ever wander away'."

Francis had resigned as the official head of the Order, but he was determined to remain its conscience. Assisted by Caesar of Speyer, he began revising his Rule for the Chapter of 1221. The document that he produced was quite long, consisting of 23 chapters, and bore little resemblance to a formal piece of monastic legislation. Rather it was more like a series of impassioned pleas by which Francis hoped to reawaken the spirit of love that had motivated his first followers. The text was replete with long quotations from the Gospel, spiritual admonitions, and prayers that attain an almost rhapsodic quality. As for the Rule itself, it included some of the reforms recently adopted, such as the one-year novitiate for entrants and the prohibition of vagabondage. In almost every other respect, however, the Rule reaffirmed as forcefully as Francis could the apostolic spirit of the original Rule of 1209. Neither individually nor collectively were the friars to own anything. They were not to claim or defend their hermitages against anyone. They were forbidden to possess or even use money. They were to travel on foot, carry nothing with them and resist not evil. They were to rejoice in the company of the poor, the weak, lepers, and beggars.

Far from mitigating the asceticism of the old Rule, the new Rule simply spelled it out in greater detail. Francis even authorized the friars to disobey any superiors who would not permit them to live according to the Gospel.

While Francis was working on the text of the new Rule, Peter of Catani died quite unexpectedly. Francis had more to rue than the death of an old and devoted friend. For the man who replaced Peter as Minister General of the Order, Brother Elias, soon became the spokesman for all those opposed to Francis' ideals of poverty and simplicity.

Not much is known about Elias' early life, but after joining the Order he proved to be a man of considerable abilities and charm. He headed the Franciscan mission to Syria in 1218, one of the very few that was successful that year. Francis apparently respected and trusted him, for Elias was one of the three brothers whom Francis took with him when he returned from the Holy Land to regain control of his Order. As long as Francis lived, Elias was somewhat restrained in his ambitions, but after Francis died, he threw aside all caution. He lived in high style, with a dozen servants and a special cook for himself, ruled the Order with an iron hand, and ruthlessly persecuted all those brothers who remained faithful to Francis' ideal. Caesar of Speyer, for example, was thrown into a dungeon where he died of ill treatment. Even Bernard of Quintavalle had to flee to escape the same fate. In 1239, Pope Gregory IX, the former Cardinal Ugolino, removed Elias from office in response to the pleas of the friars. Soon afterwards, Gregory excommunicated him.

Brother Elias was the Minister General when Francis presented his new Rule to the chapter of 1221. Francis sat at Elias' feet, pulling feebly on his tunic whenever he wished permission to speak. Sometimes Elias conveyed his words for him. For by now Francis was quite ill, and his strength was beginning to fail him. Cardinal

Ugolino was unable to attend the meeting, which was probably fortunate for him, as the proposed new Rule only incensed Elias and his followers and deepened the split within the Order. No agreement was reached on the new Rule at this meeting, and the conflict was left to Cardinal Ugolino to resolve.

Brother Elias' faction had objected chiefly to the fact that the new Rule had done nothing to ease the requirement of absolute poverty. But they also insisted, not without reason, that the document was so long and lacking in precision that it had no chance of being accepted by the Curia. As a result, Ugolino asked Francis to have another go at rewriting the Rule. The ministers directed Francis to compose a much more formal document, without lengthy quotations from the Gospel, or rapturous prayers, or ardent appeals to the friars to follow his way. In short, it was to be a dry, administrative ordinance.

Weary from the struggle to maintain his ideals, and his health declining, Francis nevertheless resumed work on a new Rule. Nothing is known of his next effort — the document was "lost" by Brother Elias, who may have been counting on time to gain his ends.

Deeply discouraged, Francis went to work again. This time he was visited by a group of Elias' followers who told him that they would never accept a Rule that ran counter to their wishes. Francis told them that he was writing under God's direction, and sent them away with a curse. One can imagine Francis' torment at seeing the rebellious friars become so bold, and his ideals openly flaunted. He told Brother Leo at this time, "This is my great grief and affliction, that in those matters that I have had confided to me by God in His mercy, some brothers are opposed to me, rendering them void and saying, 'These things are to be observed, and these not.' "

The new Rule that Francis produced was worked over considerably during long, hard negotiations with Brother Elias. Then Francis went to Rome and submitted the revised edition to Cardinal Ugolino, who gave it its final form. On November 29, 1223, it was approved by Pope Honorius and ever since has been the basic Rule of the Order.

The final Rule of 1223 bears very little resemblance to Francis' proposed Rule of 1221. It is essentially a legal document from which all of Francis' prayers and pleas for a return to the apostolic life have virtually disappeared. In fact, almost everything was removed that commanded the friars to remain truly poor, particularly the Gospel words, "Take nothing with you for your journey, neither money, nor bread, nor staff, and resist not the evildoer." Though the brothers were still required to own nothing, their vow of poverty was interpreted more and more leniently. They were able to live in comfortable residences and to have schools by means of the formula that Cardinal Ugolino had already worked out in the case of the school at Bologna

— all such buildings were the property of the Papacy and not the Friars Minor.

Despite these changes in the Rule, much of Francis' heritage has endured within the Order, and his burning idealism has continued to inspire Franciscans down through the centuries to this very day.

The Emulation of Christ

The years in which Francis saw his authority challenged and his ideals compromised were terribly painful ones for him. The gloom, however, was not unmixed. In 1221, Francis had called for another mission to Germany, and this one, led by Caesar of Speyer, had returned triumphant. The Order of Friars Minor was gradually establishing itself all over Europe and the Near East. At about the same time, a Third Order of Franciscans was rapidly taking shape. Called the Order of Penitents, it was started by Francis years before for all those men and women who wished to live in his spirit without, however, having to become monastics. These men and women, many of them married and with families, lived at home and devoted themselves to helping the poor and the sick in their communities. They were required to live modestly and simply, and to contribute their surplus income to the needy. They were also required not to take any oaths, or to bear arms, without the consent of the Pope. The refusal of the Penitents to take the usual oath of obedience to the civil authorities, and to take up arms for them when ordered, soon brought considerable persecution on the Order. As a punishment, its members were often subjected to special taxes, or forbidden to give their property to the poor. But the Order persisted, and brought about a partial disarming, at least, of the quarrelsome Italian city-states.

Though Francis probably began the Third Order as early as 1209, it did not receive a formal Rule until 1221, when Francis and Cardinal Ugolino collaborated to write one. Thereafter, the Third Order spread as rapidly throughout Europe as the Friars Minor and the Poor Ladies.

One of its early members was the Lady Jacopa de' Settesoli, a member of the Roman nobility who became a widow in 1217. She had met Francis a few years earlier, and the two struck up a great and enduring friendship. Francis often enjoyed her hospitality when in Rome, and she would make an almond confection that he seems to have relished. He called her affectionately,

"Brother Jacopa," and in gratitude for her devotion he gave her a lamb for a present. It is said that this lamb used to wake up Jacopa in the morning by gently butting her and bleating, and then would accompany her to church. From its wool, Jacopa spun and wove the habit in which Francis died.

Apart from the success of the mission to Germany and the formal establishment of the Third Order, there was very little to console Francis during this period of his greatest ordeal. He was torn by a severe conflict. Wishing as always to be an obedient son of the Church, he counseled himself to be submissive and to accept the changes in his Rule that were being pressed upon him. Sometimes he would go to extremes and say that a truly obedient man should be like a corpse. "Take a lifeless body," he would say, "and place it where you will. You will see that it does not resist being moved, it does not murmur about its position. He does not ask why he is moved, he cares not where he is placed, he does not insist on being put elsewhere."

At other times, Francis would become angry and lash out at his tormenters, saying, "Let them be accursed by You, O Lord, those men whose evil example shame the good friars of the Order and destroy by their conduct what it has pleased You to build up."

Francis was strongly tempted to authorize his loyal followers to leave the Order, but he could not bring himself to create division within the Church, and so he desisted. Finally he seems to have resolved the conflict in a way that brought him a measure of peace. He would accept the decision of the Church regarding the Rule, and resign himself to the fact that he no longer had any authority in his own Order. At the same time, he would remain faithful to the ideal of poverty and simplicity in his own life and so set an example for his brothers. There would still be times of despair when he would cry out, "Who are they who have taken away my brothers? Who are they who have stolen my family?" But the worst of his emotional ordeal was over, and he could say calmly to those brothers who sought his advice about the new Rule, "Do what you will. I am no longer obligated to do anything except pray for my friars and give them a good example."

We see what Francis meant when, at this time, he was invited to a dinner attended by important dignitaries at Cardinal Ugolino's palace. Francis first begged for his bread in the streets, and then embarrassed Cardinal Ugolino further by offering to share it with his guests. After the dinner Cardinal Ugolino reproached Francis, saying, "Brother, why do you shame me by begging alms when you are my guest? Don't you know that my house and everything in it is yours?"

Francis replied, "My Lord, nothing is more pleasing to God than Holy Poverty. Far from shaming you, should it not rather gratify you to honor in your home our Lord Christ who lived poor on earth for love of us? I must also think of my friars, present and future, who might otherwise scorn to go out begging. I must act in such a way that there will be no excuse for them not to humble themselves before God."

Not all of Francis' brothers followed his example. Thomas of Celano tells us of some who became lazy and idle:

"I wonder at the impudence of those who, according to the blessed Francis, could not have lived at home except by their sweat and now, without working, feed on the sweat of the poor. Wonderful prudence! Though they do nothing, they consider themselves always occupied. They know the hours of the meals, and if hunger takes hold of them, they complain that the sun has gone to sleep. Shall I believe, good Father [Francis], that these monsters of men are worthy of your glory? Not even of the habit!"

If the worst of Francis' emotional ordeal was over, his physical ordeal was now becoming intense. Francis' health had never been robust, even as a youth. Now the years of fasting, penances, exertions, and emotional turmoil had all taken their toll. From 1223 on, Francis was extremely ill. He was hemorrhaging internally from gastric disorders, and vomiting blood. He was also beginning to lose his sight, and suffered from severe headaches. More and more, Francis began to withdraw from the society of his Order to lead the life of a hermit, accompanied only by a few faithful friends. They were chiefly Leo, Angelo, Masseo, Rufino, and Sylvester.

Ever since his conversion, he had sought to emulate the life of Christ. Now, as he neared death, the desire to become as like Christ as possible grew even stronger. As Christmas approached, he sent for a friend, John Velita, the lord of Greccio, and a member of the Order of Penitents. Francis told him that he wished to celebrate Christ's birth "in a way to bring before me as perfectly as possible the sufferings and discomforts He endured from infancy for our salvation." Then he asked Velita to build a realistic manger on a mountain opposite Greccio, with a crib filled with hay, and an ox and a donkey. On Christmas eve, friars from all around climbed the mountain in a torchlight procession. At the Mass, Francis acted as deacon and then delivered a sermon proclaiming the joys of Heaven to all those who had faith in Jesus Christ. As he spoke of "the Child of Bethlehem," Francis' whole being was filled with love, and there were some present that night who believed that they saw the infant Jesus in the crib.

In June 1224, Francis attended the annual chapter of the friars at Assisi for the last time, and then went with his companions to Mount La Verna, the wooded peak that had been given to him years before as a place for solitude and prayer by Count Orlando. By now, Francis was too feeble to walk, and had to ride up the mountain on a mule. Near the summit, he gazed on the great beauty of the place, with its huge, moss-covered rocks, and trees of pine and beech. Then he told his companions that he believed he was near death and that he wished to remain in complete solitude "to bewail my sins before God."

Concerned about Francis' well-being, Leo nevertheless spied on him. Sometimes Leo would hear him weeping over his Order, saying, "Lord, what will become of this poor little family that You have entrusted to me when I am gone?" At other times, Leo found him conversing with God, crying out for love of Him, or rapt in ecstacy.

When Francis discovered that he was being observed, he withdrew to a ledge overhanging a chasm about 120 feet deep. There he began a fast that lasted several days, all the while praying with even greater ardor than before. Just before sunrise on September 14, 1224, he prayed fervently to experience before he died the pain that Christ had suffered on the Cross and the love that had made Him sacrifice Himself for mankind. Afterwards, a vision appeared to Francis of an angel whose features bore the likeness of Jesus Christ. The angel fixed his gaze on Francis, and then left him.

When Francis returned to his brothers, he bore the wounds that Christ had suffered on the Cross. His hands and feet appeared to have been pierced with nails, and blood flowed from a wound on his side. Francis kept the wounds covered, but a number of people were able to see them, including Brother Leo, who nursed them for him. At Francis' death, the wounds were still visible, though black and swollen, "as nailheads in the flesh," according to Brother Elias. These wounds were seen by many and believed in. Pope Alexander IV stated that he had personally seen the marks on Francis while the saint was still alive. How the marks of the Stigmata were formed we cannot know. But to Francis' followers, it was an event completely in keeping with his life. Francis, who had so profoundly imitated Christ in his faith, had achieved a material transformation, a miracle upon his own body. "The mind," wrote St. Bonaventura, one of Francis' early biographers, "became apparent in the flesh."

The joy of receiving the Stigmata did much to buoy Francis' spirits and relieve his inner torment. A few days later, he left Mount La Verna and, accompanied only by Brother Leo, began the journey back to the Portiuncula. He now had to travel constantly on a donkey. The trip rapidly became a triumphal procession. Leo had made no secret of the miracle that had taken place on La Verna, and everywhere crowds came to see and touch Francis, for it was believed that such contact could effect miraculous cures. In his dazed and weakened condition, and nearly blind by this time, Francis was often unaware of the crowds. Yet such adulation always caused him great discomfort. On one occasion, a holy day on which eating meat was proscribed, Francis told the crowds, "You have come here because you think that I am so pious and God-fearing. Therefore I must tell you that on this fast day I have eaten food that was prepared with lard." (Francis' gastric disorders required him to eat food cooked with lard, rather than oil.)

Francis was utterly incapable of dishonesty or hypocrisy. Once the brothers persuaded him to wear a piece of fur inside his tunic to keep him warmer in the winter. He agreed on one condition — that a piece of fur be sewed on the outside of the tunic too so that all could see what he was doing.

The Death of Il Poverello

o sooner was Francis back at the Portiuncula than it seemed that all the missionary zeal of his youth returned. Riding his donkey, he would visit four or five towns a day and preach in them. For a while he thought it was not too late to make a fresh start and still accomplish great things. The thought of going back again among the lepers to serve them also occurred to him. Unfortunately, it was all wishful thinking. Francis was dying, and he had little strength for new ventures now. Both Brother Elias and Cardinal Ugolino were urging him to seek medical help, but Francis had little faith in doctors. Instead, he decided to seek seclusion and rest at

San Damiano. There Clare had a reed hut built for him and nursed him for several weeks. At first it seemed that he would not survive. Then he had to endure the agonizing experience of having his hut overrun by field mice that swarmed all over him at night. Is it any wonder that he sometimes wept for hours?

But gradually Clare, helped by Leo, Angelo, and Rufino, was able to restore some of his strength and revive his good spirits. After awhile, Francis could be heard singing again. In his joy and gratitude for surviving, he wrote a song in which he thanked God for having created all nature and life. He called it "The Canticle of Brother Sun." Its words are considered one of the most beautiful religious poems ever written. Francis dictated them first, and then adapted a melody for it. He wanted his friars to sing it everywhere like troubadours. Here are its words:

Most High Almighty Good Lord,
Yours are praise, glory, honor, and all
   blessing.
To You alone, Most High, do they belong,
And no man is worthy to mention You.

Be praised, my Lord, with all Your creatures,
Especially Sir Brother Sun,
Who is daylight, and by him You shed light
   on us.
And he is beautiful and radiant with great
   splendor.
Of You, Most High, he is a symbol.

Be praised, my Lord, from Sister Moon and
    the Stars.
In heaven You have formed them clear and
    bright and fair.

Be praised, my Lord, from Brother Wind
And from air and cloud and clear and all
    weather,
By which You give Your creatures nourish-
    ment.

Be praised, my Lord, from Sister Water,
For she is very useful, humble, precious,
    and pure.

Be praised, my Lord, from Brother Fire,
By whom You light up the night,
For he is fair and merry and mighty and
    strong.

Be praised, my Lord, from our Sister Mother
    Earth,
Who sustains and rules us
And produces varied fruits and many-
    colored flowers and plants.

Praise and bless my Lord
And give Him thanks and serve Him with
    great humility.

As soon as Francis was well enough, he set
out for Rieti, about 50 miles south, where Pope
Honorius and Cardinal Ugolino were staying at
the time. Once again he was the object of almost
frenzied veneration. At Rieti, people fought over

pieces of his clothes, strands of his hair, and even cuttings from his nails. Francis had become a living relic. Meanwhile Cardinal Ugolino pressed Francis to consult the Pope's physicians about his growing blindness. He acceded, and received the eminent doctors at the nearby hermitage of Fonte Columbo. The treatment they recommended was to burn one of his temples from the ear to the eyebrow with a red hot iron. As the doctors approached with the glowing iron, Francis shuddered and then said, "Brother Fire, the Lord has made you strong and beautiful and useful. I have always loved you, so now be courteous and gentle to me."

After the doctors had seared his temple with the iron, another doctor saw fit to pierce his ears with it. Francis endured this agony bravely, and even chided those brothers who had run away rather than witness it.

In the early spring of 1226, Francis went to Siena, which was noted both for its mild climate and its esteemed physicians. The doctors there were no more helpful than the Pope's physicians. One night, in fact, Francis vomited so much blood that he and the friars were sure that death was imminent. Brother Elias hastened to his bedside. Elias, like most Assisians, was afraid that Francis might die away from home and his body seized as a relic by "foreigners." (Perugia especially was feared in this respect.) The relics of holy men were greatly prized during the Middle Ages. They were venerated by the devout, they were thought to work miracles, and they brought a city both prestige and profit from the visits of pilgrims. Therefore an armed guard was sent from Assisi to protect the invalid on his way home.

Led by Brother Elias, the knights took a circuitous route. At one village, they could not buy food. Francis laughed at them and told them to beg for it. The villagers gladly gave it to them.

Francis received a triumphant welcome in Assisi. "Everybody," Thomas of Celano wrote, "exulted, for they hoped that the saint would soon die, and they blessed God for bringing him back to their city."

It was deemed unsafe to leave Francis at the Portiuncula — the place was too exposed to enemy raids. Instead Francis was brought to Bishop Guido's palace where tight security precautions were taken to prevent a kidnapping.

On his sickbed, Francis dictated a number of messages that he wished to be preserved and kept on record after his death. In one of these, he described the qualities that the ideal Minister General of the Order should possess:

"If he is a scholar, far from priding himself on his learning, let him be diligent above all to be humble and simple, endeavoring to preach by example rather than by word. And let him not be a collector of books, lest study make him neglect the duties of his office. As the head of a family of poor men whose model he is to be, let him hate money, convinced that there is no greater corrupter for us, no deadlier foe."

Perhaps Francis was already concerned about

how Brother Elias might behave after he (Francis) died.

A doctor friend visited Francis at the palace and, prodded by the invalid to be truthful, told him that his disease was incurable and that death was only a matter of weeks away. For a moment Francis was silent. Then he stretched his arms upward and cried out, "Welcome, Sister Death!" Soon after, he composed the last verse of "The Canticle of Brother Sun":

Be praised, my Lord, from our Sister Bodily
    Death,
From whom no living man can escape.
Woe to those who die in mortal sin.
Blessed are they whom she shall find in
    Your most holy will,
For the second death shall not harm them.

Francis asked Leo and Angelo to sing this stanza several times a day with him, and even at night, "to comfort him and to entertain the armed guard in front of the palace."

Brother Elias was shocked by the sound of singing in the palace where Francis was dying. He told Francis, in effect, that this was hardly the way people expected a saint to die. Francis had been submissive for a long time, but this was too much. He felt he might at least be permitted to die in his own fashion. So he told Elias, "Leave me be, Brother. For I feel so close to God that I may well be allowed to sing and rejoice!"

If Francis expected to die at any moment, it

is quite understandable. By this time he was thoroughly emaciated by disease, barely more than skin and bones. His suffering was acute. He told a brother that "the cruelest martyrdom would be easier to bear than three days of pain like this."

Yet Francis somehow endured for a few more weeks, and he used that time to write his Last Will and Testament. It is a remarkable document, this farewell to his brothers, in which he restates with eloquent simplicity the beliefs by which he had lived.

He tells first of his early life, "When I was yet in my sins and it seemed unbearably bitter to me to look upon lepers." Then he recalls, "The sweetness of soul" that came to him with conversion, his great reverence for priests and the sacrament of Communion, and the joys of the early years of his Order. Then the friars "were content with one habit, with a cord, and breeches. And we had no desire for anything else, and quite willingly we would live in poor and abandoned churches."

After looking back, Francis thinks of the future, and speaks out for the last time against the changes being made in his Order. He forbids the friars "to receive churches, houses, and all else built for their use, unless these are truly in keeping with Holy Poverty." Later he "firmly commands" the friars that "they do not dare ask for any letter of privilege" from the Papacy, "not even as protection against persecution."

Following a passage in which he states his

"firm desire" to be obedient, he closes with these sentences:

"And the friars should not say, 'This is another Rule,' because this is a reminder of the past, an admonition and exhortation, and my testament, which I, little Brother Francis, am making for you, my blessed brothers, so that we may observe in a more catholic way the Rule we have promised the Lord. And the Minister General and all other ministers shall be bound by obedience not to add to these words or take away from them. And let them always have this writing with them together with the Rule, and in all the chapters they hold, when they read the Rule, let them read these words also. And all my brothers I firmly charge by obedience not to make any interpretations of the Rule or of these words and say, 'They are to be understood thus.' Rather, as the Lord has granted me simply and plainly to speak and write the Rule and these words, so simply you are to understand them and by holy deeds carry them out until the very end."

Apparently Francis still hoped to restore his ideals of absolute poverty and simplicity in the Order he founded by means of this Testament, which, he hoped, would supplement the Rule of 1223. However, it was not to be. Four years after Francis' death, Pope Gregory IX, the former Cardinal Ugolino, settled the matter by telling the friars that Francis' Testament was not legally binding on them. The struggle between those who wished to live according to Francis' ideal and those who wished to follow the much more moderate Rule of 1223 continued, however, for a century.

Having written his Last Will and Testament reaffirming his faith, Francis now had only to await death. He wished to spend his last days in the peaceful surroundings of his beloved Portiuncula, and the magistrates of Assisi gave their consent. Accompanied by an armed escort, he was borne through the streets of the city, which Francis blessed for the last time. Then, at the Portiuncula, he was settled in a hut a few feet from the chapel, an appropriate setting for his death.

To Clare, he sent a final message, and bade her not to grieve for him. His message said, "I, little Brother Francis, wish to follow the life and poverty of our Lord Jesus Christ and of His most holy Mother, and to persevere in it to the end. And I beg you, my Ladies, whatever advice you may receive in the future, never to depart from it."

Francis then expressed a desire to see Lady Jacopa before he died. In a note that he dictated to her, he asked her "to bring whatever is necessary for my burial." Then, with the whimsy of a sick man, he added, "And please bring with you also some of the good things you gave me to eat when I was ill in Rome."

It wasn't necessary to send the note. Lady Jacopa had heard that he was dying and had hastened to the Portiuncula herself with everything required for his funeral. She even brought with her the almond confection that he loved. Though women were not allowed at the Portiuncula, Francis ordered that she be let in. "God be praised," he said. "The ban on women entering here is not for Brother Jacopa." She remained to watch over him until the very end.

On October 1, 1226, Francis bade the brothers to place him on the ground naked, for he wished to die in true poverty. Later he blessed them, beginning with Bernard of Quintavalle, his first disciple. The next day he broke bread with them, just as Christ had done with his disciples. On October 3, after again being placed on the ground wrapped in a coarse cloth, he intoned a Psalm and then breathed his last. "All the mysteries of Christ being fulfilled in him," Thomas of Celano wrote, "he winged his way happily to God." Francis was 46 years old.

The next day, a Sunday, a procession was formed to bear Francis' body to the church of San Giorgio in Assisi for burial. In accordance with his wishes, the procession stopped first at San Damiano, so that Clare could see him for the last time. According to one biographer, "She bathed the holy corpse with her tears and covered the sacred Stigmata with kisses."

Within two years after his death, Francis was proclaimed a saint of the Church in ceremonies presided over by Pope Gregory IX. At the same time, Gregory authorized Brother Elias to build a great church in Assisi in honor of the saint. On May 25, 1230, Francis' body was transferred to a crypt in this new church. The basilica that Brother Elias erected in Francis' memory is truly magnificent. Its walls and ceilings were later enhanced by frescoes painted by the great 14th-century artist, Giotto, depicting scenes from Francis' life. Some who see the basilica may feel that the founder of the Order of Friars Minor deserved no less. Others, however, may find it inappropriate for such a saint as Il Poverello.

Yet the most enduring monument to St. Francis will always be his spirit. It is the spirit of a basically simple, almost unlettered man who understood better than any other man of his time or later that *all* of God's creation is worthy of love, reverence, and preservation. In his own words of greeting to all, *Pax et Bonum* (Peace and Goodness).

BIBLIOGRAPHY

Boase, T.S. *St. Francis of Assisi.* Indiana University Press, 1968.

Chesterton, Gilbert K. *Saint Francis of Assisi.* Image Books, 1957.

Cuthbert, Father. *Life of Saint Francis of Assisi.* Verry, 1960.

Englebert, Abbe Omer. *Saint Francis of Assisi.* Franciscan Herald Press, 1965.

Hegener, Fr. Mark. *The Poverello: St. Francis of Assisi.* Franciscan Herald Press, 1956.

Jorgensen, Johannes. *St. Francis of Assisi.* Image Books, 1955.

Robeck, Nesta de. *Saint Francis.* Casa Editrice Francescana, 1967.

Sabatier, Paul. *The Life of St. Francis of Assisi.* Charles Scribner's Sons, 1938.

Thomas of Celano. *Brother Saint Francis of Assisi.* Franciscan Herald Press, 1962.